Permission to Dream

I CAN ~ I WILL ~ I DID

Thomas R. Williams

with Kathleen Birmingham

THOMAS R. WILLIAMS, INC.

LOS ANGELES, CALIFORNIA

Thomas R. Williams/Thomas R. Williams, Inc.
578 Washington Boulevard, #428
Marina del Rey, CA 90292
www.ThomasRWilliams.com

Book Layout ©2013 BookDesignTemplates.com
Photos: Manda Aiello Photography
Cover Design: Kelly Pion-Capone-The K Factor Enterprises; Scott Capone-Capone Strategies, Inc.

For Quantity Sales, Ordering Information, Speaking Engagement Information:
Please go to www.ThomasRWilliams.com/contacts.html

Permission to Dream/ Thomas R. Williams. —1st ed.
ISBN 978-0-9905374-0-3

Contents

Dedication:

To my mom for never giving up on me, who told me at a young age, "You can be anything you want to be," and I was ignorant enough to actually believe her!

To every person young or old, you can turn your dreams into a reality. Dreams don't have an expiration date. If you want to do something go for it! You don't have to settle for mediocrity.
Strive for greatness.

I truly believe to my core that anyone, anytime, anywhere can become anything they want to be.
There is a time and place for anything.
The time is NOW and the place is HERE!

Foreword

I am a former football coach and currently a high school principal. The jobs are very similar and I'm honored to have had two such important jobs. Both have the same goals. We take the students who show up at our campus or on our field, we figure out the puzzle that defines them, and we work very hard to create the best version of them that they can be. It's that simple and it's very, very tough to do. Some have extraordinary talent. Some have big dreams. Some have extraordinary talent and no dreams. Some have baggage that gets in their way every day. As educators, it's our job to figure out the puzzle that makes up each individual and put them on a path to dream big and achieve their biggest goals.

Thomas Williams was quite a puzzle. At first glance, he had it all. He was big, strong, fast, smart, and had a swagger about him that exuded confidence. All this I learned just from watching him play little league baseball. He was a legend among the little league players. He was an imposing player with legendary results. He threw hard and hit harder. As Thomas approached his freshman year in high school, it was easy for me to see Thomas as a great football player in our program. He had a different picture of his high school years. He was a "baseball only" guy and not interested in football. We had several discussions about that decision before he arrived here. I had three excellent reasons why he should play football his freshman year. First, I'm a football coach and a better one when I have outstanding athletes who are fast, strong, and hard working. That was the selfish part for me. Second, I believe that high school students should play multiple sports. They improve in their main sport if they play others. It's a philosophy we've had here for many years and it has served us well. Lastly, Thomas would be part of something in high school right away. We spend much time and money connecting our freshmen to something at school. I figured Thomas would be better at football than raising pigs with our FFA group.

The good news about the multiple conversations I had with Thomas is that I learned a lot about the puzzle that was Thomas. I learned that he didn't have the extreme confidence that he showed on the baseball field. He actually was hesitant about his abilities. I also learned that Thomas had a huge fear of failure and this resonated with me. I am like that. I just don't want to mess up the good things we have going at Vacaville High School. It drives me and I noticed it drove Thomas as well. He wasn't sure about freshmen football, but he played and was successful. The next year we decided to bring Thomas to the varsity in his sophomore year. Again, he resisted. He wanted to stay with his friends and play junior varsity. By then I knew that Thomas had some big dreams and I couldn't let him derail those dreams by playing it safe. We convinced him to stay with the varsity and supported him all the way. He needed extra time and attention to feel comfortable competing at the varsity level, and he succeeded. Then, I learned the final piece of the puzzle about Thomas and he soared from there.

Thomas Williams is willing to out-work everyone else to achieve his big dreams. Every day at football he would stay after to ask "one more question" or "practice one more drill." He asked every day. He was a workout junkie. He would lift with his team. He would lift on his own and then he would run hills in the extreme heat of Vacaville. He never wasted a day. He also figured out very early on that he needed the same intensity in the classroom. He connected his academics with his athletics and that's something that some outstanding athletes never figure out. Thomas was not a naturally gifted student. He was, however, the hardest worker in the class. Some of his teachers originally thought he was "playing" them for a grade but then they realized it was his extreme desire to succeed that pushed him to ask for extra help and more opportunities to learn. Thomas Williams figured out that big secret of whether you're the best at something or middle of the pack; hard work and determination allow you to achieve big.

In addition to hard work and determination, we have learned together that a strong focus is necessary as well. Thomas had a million possible distractions. There were the normal temptations of high school like dating, parties, and other fun things that distract from the main goal. He confidently avoided those because he knew that would diminish all of his previous hard work. He had additional distractions of the recruiting process. Wow, did coaches show up day after day to chat with Thomas. It's a scary process to watch. It sure would be easy to think you're great and don't have to continue to work with every coach around telling you how great you are and how well you'll do at their school. Thomas never was distracted by that attention. He knew what it was and he was humble but continued to work hard. He even asked that he not be taken out of certain classes that he felt he needed to be in every day. It was a maturity that made me proud.

Through the years Thomas has given me some credit for his success. I am humbled by that but I believe what I've learned from Thomas has helped so many students and athletes after him. I'm known as a bit of a nag around this school for pushing kids to take harder classes and participate in more activities. We encourage trying to take an AP class or to take a fourth year of math and science.

We preach that we are willing to out-work everyone else. We come on Saturdays and learn. We come early and stay late to learn. We now have many examples of students who have bought in to this formula and Thomas gets much credit for showing us what's possible. Thomas has shown us what can happen when we combine our natural gifts with a focus and determination to succeed. It is my job and the job of every educator and coach to give every student the permission to dream . . . and the tools to achieve those dreams.

Ed Santopadre, Principal
Vacaville High School, Vacaville California
June 21, 2014

Preface

As I sit and write to you, thoughts of critical moments in my life come to mind. I need to share with you something I figured out:

In life, we are given circumstances and situations that have the power to transcend our lives.

As a little boy, I often hid my feelings, especially during the times in my life when things weren't so perfect. In fact, in my eyes, they were downright bad. I would hide my tears when I got teased about my mother cleaning houses for a living, or that I didn't have normal hair. It hurt growing up without a father. It embarrassed me to have to wear clothes that were out of style because they were the only ones we could afford. Sometimes I hated people, lashing out at them so that they would feel some of the pain I felt.

I asked, "Why me, God?"

Yet I was more than happy to accept any of the good things in life that came my way. My grandparents, who gave us a home, loved and supported us after my parents divorced. I had an entire community who wrapped their arms around me and helped me grow from an angry boy to a better man. I had coaches who taught me discipline, accountability, and respect. There were teachers who took time to meet with me before and after school helping me overcome my lack of knowledge. I had friends who welcomed me into their homes, treating me like family. I can see them now as the blessings they were. At the time, I took it all for granted.

But good things in life don't come without the bad. They're a package. I was shaped by my experiences.

The GOOD made me.

The BAD made me.

There were many times I thought that life would be so much easier if we just had a little more money. But learning to make do with what we had gave me character and I appreciated what I earned more than if it had just been given to me.

"Perfect" doesn't make you strong.

Overcoming obstacles is what makes you strong.

Instead of focusing on the humiliating things in my life, I now look at each experience and wonder what life is teaching me for the future. I model myself after the coaches and teachers who mentored, taught, and corrected me because I want to be more like them.

My life will be what I make of it. Every single one of us has the ability to learn from our past and have HOPE for our future. It wasn't until the moment I gave myself *Permission to Dream* that I was free.

Once I understood this, my entire perspective on life changed. The father I missed so much growing up was there for me when I went to college. He saw me play several games at USC and many more in the NFL. We both learned to "live in the moment" of our relationship, not going back to the past. As a result, I have a fantastic relationship with my dad. We talk almost every day. He is the reason I have my relationship with God the way that I do. Looking back on my childhood, this is nothing short of a miracle.

Every single person reading this book is on a journey and it is as individual as you are, so embrace it. No matter where you are on your path, never compare yourself to someone else. Keep looking at your life as the training ground for your future. The lessons you have experienced in your past have helped you become the person you are today and will lead you to becoming a better person in the future.

Know that some of those tough times in your past were preparing you for the challenge you may face tomorrow. You'll wake up one day and say, "Oh, NOW I understand!" Leave all regrets in the past. Everyone has made mistakes. The longer we carry that kind of baggage around with us, the heavier it becomes. That's what limits us. By learning and growing from our mistakes, we have the knowledge and the ability to move ahead.

I want to reach out to all of you who are teachers, mentors, coaches, and parents. Give our youth every chance they deserve. If they are acting out, try to figure out why. I didn't know why I was acting out as a child. Fortunately I had just the right people at various times in my life who believed in me enough to make me WANT to change.

Your words are incredibly powerful. The instant you tell a child, "You can't." They believe you. And, the instant you encourage them by saying, "You can," they believe that too.

At one time in your life, you may have had your dream crushed. Someone planted a seed in your mind allowing you to think that you might not be good enough to live your dream. I'm here to tell you that it isn't too late to start believing in your dream again. Here's the truth, it's never too late. Not for you. Not for that child in your home, your class, or on your team.

Giving that child hope for their future is your job. There are enough dream stealers in the world. Be a dream maker. Too many of our youth believe that they have no hope for a better life. I thought that too. But once I changed my belief and began to see myself as a professional athlete, working hard on that dream, my entire life changed.

As a parent, mentor, coach, or teacher, you have such an important responsibility. Encourage and support a child's vision. Start as young as possible, but know they're never too old to start either. The more a child hears they can do something, the more they will believe it.

Help them figure out their dream, no matter how unrealistic it may seem to be. You hold the key to the infinite amount of greatness contained inside each child you serve. Give those children *Permission to Dream* and they will find within themselves the courage and passion they need to make it come true.

Sincerely,
Thomas R. Williams

Acknowledgments

Mom, I thank you for everything that you sacrificed in order for me to dream. And thank you for telling me at a young age, I can grow up to be anything I wanted to be. I only pray that I can be half the parent to my child that you were to me. Your confidence, words, and encouragement have meant so much to me. I can honestly say; because you believed in my dream, so too, did I.

My grandparents, thank you for taking us in during my very young and important developmental years. There was so much that I was exposed to during those years that I still hold on to as valuable lessons to this day.

Dad, thank you for the relationship we have today. Our conversations over the years have helped me through some of the toughest times in my life. I love you, man.

Ron, you came into my life at the most perfect time. You gave me a male role model to look up to when I didn't have one. You are a true definition of what it is to be a MAN. THANK YOU.

Coach Santopadre, thank you for all our talks and for listening to me. Thank you for giving me an environment that allowed me to be vulnerable enough to tell you my deepest fears and biggest dreams.

Because of coaches and teachers like you, students around the world have permission to dream.

Kelly and Scott, thank you for being such a huge part of my transition. Without your help, I would not have the amount of success that I have. You are great team members that allow TRW, Inc. to operate on all cylinders.

Vacaville, there are so many of you that I thank. It is because of your collective involvement in my life that I have turned out to be the man I am today. You really showed me that it *takes a village to raise a child.*

CHAPTER 1

It Wasn't Me . . . I Swear

I heard the exasperation in the words, as I did every time. "Thomas, you're here again?"

My principal, Mr. Watson, and I were becoming very good friends my first year at Cooper Elementary in Vacaville, California.

We frequently met in his office, Mr. Watson behind his desk fingers laced; me in a hard blue plastic chair before him. I scooted back in the uncomfortable chair, putting my arms up on the armrests, nonchalantly, I thought. Then I noticed my feet sticking out in front of me, so I scooted to the front edge of the chair which allowed the heels of my sneakers to kick the scuffed steel legs.

Neither position felt particularly powerful, but as I coolly met Mr. Watson's gaze, I didn't let it show that he intimidated me.

I wondered what the kids back in class were thinking of my achievement on the playground.

Principal Watson's voice droned comfortably as I daydreamed. Suddenly it developed a hard edge forcing me to pay attention. "Thomas, the only thing I can do is call your mother." His eyes bore into mine. "Again."

"Mom's not home."

"Then I'll call your grandmother." With that he dialed the phone.

1

I stood mute.

I'd won.

Young as I was, I knew Principal Watson expected me to show contrition for starting yet another fight on the playground. I don't think he understood exactly how hard that was to do. My very presence in his office established the sway of power.

I was someone.

I wasn't invisible.

But I was in trouble. Again.

At this point in my life, I had learned that if I wanted something, the only one who was going to get it for me . . . was me.

And sometimes the only way I could get it was to fight for it.

At the age of six, I knew I wanted people to see me, to pay attention to me.

And I really didn't care exactly how I got that attention.

⚬ᕤᘰ ᘺᕤ⚬

My mother came from the Bay Area, Walnut Creek, California. She had joined the military to get out of the house after high school, looking for some sort of independence.

My father came from thousands of miles away, a town called Dillon in South Carolina.

They met in the army at Fort Riley, Kansas. That was roughly halfway across the country for both of them.

They fell in love, got married, and had me.

Two years after I was born, Dad was transferred to Fort Gordon in Georgia.

Being that I was born in Fort Riley, Kansas, about halfway between California and South Carolina, my life made a strange kind of sense.

Mom was white.

Dad was black.

So I figured that made me a compromise, half-black, half-white, born about halfway between their two hometowns.

And before you even have to ask, yes, that caused problems for me growing up.

It was an identity crisis, only I didn't know enough to call it that. At six I couldn't figure out where I belonged. To the white world or to the black world?

No one ever thought to tell me how to navigate that uncharted territory, so I just pushed ahead in the only way I knew.

At school, I usually used force.

I was bigger than most kids. For the time being, that worked. At home, however, I had to use my innate charm and cuteness. It didn't work every time, but it worked often enough to keep in my bag of tricks.

∼⊙ℓ ℓ⊙∼

By the time I was four years old, Mom and Dad realized that there weren't enough compromises to save their marriage. They divorced and went back to their respective corners of the country.

Actually, Dad was transferred to Germany and Mom took this as a sign that it was time to cut her losses and moved back home.

I was too young to understand. Some time later I remember her saying, "The damage has already been done. There will never be a reconciliation." They had exhausted time and possibilities by that point.

As a result, I became a California boy with a serious chip on my shoulder because even at my age, I knew that people looked at me and judged me.

I'd be in McDonald's with Mom and I watched as people looked at me, and then looked at my mom. I could read in their faces just as clearly as if they'd said it out loud, "What's that pretty white woman doing with a black boy?"

At first I ignored it, because until you're a certain age you don't notice people pointing at you and whispering. But it happened over and over again. Even a kid as thick-headed as I was started to notice.

Who was I?

Was I really that different?

At my Parent-Teacher conference with Mom in the fall of first-grade, my friends and classmates would ask, "Who's that with you, Thomas?"

"That's my mom." I always said this with pride. I had a great mom.

"That can't be your mom! She's white. You're black."

What did that really mean? Of course she was my mom. I knew I wasn't the best student in the first grade, but some of the kids in my class didn't seem all that bright to me. Who else would be coming to Parent-Teacher conference if she weren't my mom?

One day at recess I got another clue.

A certain group of kids in my class were the cool kids. At least from my perspective, these kids were cooler than me.

They wore cool clothes.

They had cool shoes.

And they had the coolest haircuts. I wanted to be cool too, so I asked Bobby, "Hey, how do you get your hair to look so cool and spiky?"

"You kidding? I just use gel and water." He walked over to the drinking fountain, got his hands wet and transferred the water to his hair. A few quick movements were all he needed. When Bobby took his hands away, his hair was perfectly spiked.

Now that's what I was talking about.

"Let me try." I got my hair wet and mussed it up the way Bobby had done. Only it didn't work for me the way it had for him.

"Hey, Thomas! You just have weird hair!" Not exactly fighting words, but I wasn't going to just stand there and let someone make fun of me. My dad taught me better than that.

"What's wrong with my hair?" As I looked at the other first grade boys I noticed that they all had lighter hair. And their hair was straight, straight, straight. I put a hand up to my head and felt the coarse springy curls closely hugging my scalp.

"Thomas has a poodle on his head!"

"No, it's a scrubbing pad from the kitchen!"

"Hey Brillo Pad! What's up?"

That was it. No one made fun of me. I threw one punch and that started everything. Pretty soon we were on the ground going at it in the time-honored tradition of young males. As we wrestled with one another, Bobby's face got red. We were both yelling and screaming.

Things escalated fast with me.

One thing I did remember my dad saying was that I had a right to stand up for myself.

At first the rest of the boys stood around in shock. Then they closed ranks and ganged up against me, trying to pull me off Bobby.

That left me no choice; I knocked a couple more boys down before I heard the loud voice of the principal just as his big, heavy hand grabbed my shoulder.

"That's enough, young man! Thomas! Stop!"

I struggled against his grip until I realized that no one else was coming at me.

Along we trotted, straight to the office where I had another heart-to-to heart with Mr. Watson.

"Thomas, weren't you just in here yesterday?"

Being in a one-on-one conversation with adults was pretty natural for me, so I settled in for our chat. Today Mr. Watson just glared at me, shook his head and dialed the phone. It looked to me as if he only pushed a button or two.

Way to go, Thomas. Mr. Watson has you on speed-dial.

After a terse conversation he hung up the phone and with a swift movement of his hand he indicated that our friendly chat was over for the day.

I followed the direction of his thumb and left his office. There I waited for Grandma to come and pick me up.

Anytime Grandma had to come to school to collect me, her eyes were always a little sad. By the time she arrived, I knew she was disappointed in me. I felt bad about that, but no one was going to make fun of me.

We walked across the street in silence and just as we entered the house I shouted, "I hate my hair!"

Grandma looked at me in surprise. "What's wrong with your hair?"

"I want it to be straight. Or in a spike like Bobby's hair."

Grandma nodded her head as if she understood. Then she came close and put her hands gently on my shoulders. "Thomas, your hair doesn't grow that way."

That was not what I wanted to hear. I wanted to be one of the cool kids. They all had straight, spiky hair.

"What's wrong with this? I LIKE your hair that way."

Still not what I wanted to hear.

I went into the bathroom and stared at myself in the mirror. I had green-hazel eyes like my mom, but my hair was black and curly.

Grandma came up behind me. She put her arms around my shoulders and hugged me as she met my eyes in the mirror. "Let's play with it a little." She took the comb, got my hair wet, and tried to straighten my tightly woven curls.

We could both see it wasn't working.

"Well, I like your hair. But if it would make you feel better, we can have you go with Papa and get your hair cut at Barber Joe's.

Going with Grandpa to the barbershop sounded like a good idea. Maybe I just needed the right person to cut my hair.

Still gazing into the mirror, I wasn't looking at my hair now, but at Grandma. I noticed again that Grandma's skin was white against my very brown skin. No wonder people looked at us funny. I didn't look anything like my mom or my grandmother.

When I didn't think about it, it didn't bother me. But after the fight on the playground, it was pounded in yet again that I was half-black, half-white.

And to make matters worse, I only had half a family because all the kids at school had both a dad and a mom.

All the kids, that is, but me.

I had Mom, and Grandma, and Papa, my step-granddad.

What I didn't have was a dad to play catch with, to wrestle with, to do "guy things" with.

Those thoughts, however, I kept to myself.

Grandma sent me to my room. "You think about what happened today, Thomas. You can't just go around giving people a bloody nose."

"But Grandma, they made fun of my hair." How could she not understand? Besides, I hadn't given anyone a bloody nose.

"They were just teasing you, Thomas. Remember, sticks and stones."

She stopped as I interrupted her. "Yeah, yeah, I know." But their words did hurt. They made me feel like they were better than I was.

But how? What made them better?

Being alone wasn't comfortable to me, so after just a few minutes, I sidled to the door, poked my head out and put on the cutest face I knew. "Grandma, can I come out of my room now? I've learned my lesson. I promise I won't do it again."

"Thomas, you'll be the end of me." She pretended to be exasperated, but we both knew she couldn't resist the sad puppy-dog look on my face.

"Come on out, then. But this had better be the last time."

We both knew it wouldn't be.

CHAPTER 2

Doing It My Way

Mom came home from work and we all ate the dinner Grandma had prepared.

"Thomas had to come home again today." Grandma put a fork of food in her mouth and chewed, looking down at her plate as she cut her next bite.

No help there.

"Oh, Thomas." Mom's face wore the stress of every long hour she had spent cleaning the houses of other people. I felt the tiniest niggle of regret. She shouldn't have to worry about me.

By now Grandma had swallowed her bite of food and came to my rescue. "Don't worry, I think Thomas knows better now, don't you?"

I nodded as she looked at me. With any luck, I wouldn't have to go to my room and write a hundred times that I would behave.

"Well, I hope so," Mom said. Her voice was low and she didn't look at me. She was exhausted and me being sent home from school was just another burden for her to bear.

At bedtime, I had a routine.

I was supposed to brush my teeth before going to bed and on a list of favorite things, brushing teeth wasn't high on it. It wasn't on it at all.

So, I skipped it.

"Goodnight, Papa." I gave my grandfather a hug and then moved over to my grandma. "Goodnight, Grandma."

She looked at me over the rims of her glasses, her eyes squinted in suspicion. "Did you brush your teeth?"

I gave her my sweet 'I'm so innocent' smile and shook my head from side to side. "No. I didn't. Would you do it for me?"

"Thomas, you know that if you don't brush your teeth they're going to fall right out of your head!" Yet, even as she said this, she got up and with a hand on my shoulder, guided me to the hall bathroom. There she picked up my green toothbrush, applied a pebble of toothpaste and said, "Open up."

She could have really scrubbed hard, hurting me in her irritation, but Grandma wasn't like that. She loved me. Sometimes I felt a little guilty about manipulating her, but I loved having her take care of me, almost like I was still a baby.

Once I spit out the bubbles and rinsed my mouth, I gave her a big hug. "Goodnight, Grandma. I love you."

Her arms were soft and warm as she hugged me. "I love you too, Thomas. Now get to bed."

For some kids, that would have been it, but I had one more thing I had to do, and this time it wasn't about trying to get my way about something.

"Mom?"

"Yes, Thomas?" Mom helped me put out my clothes for the next day, then turned to choose what she would wear the next day to prepare for the morning.

"Did you lock the door?"

She smiled, as she did every night when I asked her that question. "Yes, Hon. I did. It's locked. We're safe and sound."

I still had to go to the bedroom door and check. Sure enough, it was locked. I checked that the window was closed and locked as well.

After we turned out the lights I lay in the darkness of the room.

I knew that Mom thought I was afraid of someone or something coming in and scaring me. I couldn't get her to understand that I really wasn't scared about much. Kids at school teased each other about the Boogie-Man, but I knew I could take care of myself. I'd just punch him until he realized that he didn't want to mess with the kid in this house.

What I was afraid of was something happening to my mom. My memories of her tears had only gotten stronger since we'd moved to California. Her screams of terror and pain often filled my dreams and in those dreams I wasn't able to take care of her.

Before we moved to California to live with Mom's parents, our family life had been quite a roller coaster.

When things went well, I had loved our family life, what I could remember of being a family with Mom and Dad.

But my dad liked to drink.

And when he had too much to drink, he liked to use his hands. It made sense; he had been a boxer before he went into the army, and once a man learns to use his hands, well that's pretty much what he knows.

My dad was actually an amateur boxing champion and would fight throughout the week. He was on the army boxing team and he traveled with them.

What I couldn't really understand was when Dad would use his hands on Mom.

The first time I ever got up during the night when I heard their raised voices, I'd crept down the hall to the living room where they were screaming at each other. But the instant Mom saw me, she stopped and held up her hand to my dad, trying to get him to stop.

"Stop T.R.!" Mom's voice shook.

Dad grabbed her wrist as she tried to defend herself and I could tell from her gasp of pain and the weird way her voice sounded that it wasn't a game.

"Thomas, honey, go back to bed. Go on now. Everything will be fine."

Only it wasn't fine.

I had obeyed Mom, tiptoeing down the hall to my room, but the sounds of blows, flesh against flesh, continued. Mom's cries of pain and fear kept me from sleeping.

It was only after everything got quiet that I finally went to sleep.

On the mornings after their fight, Mom's eyes were puffy and red. She'd kiss and hug me and tell me everything would be better tomorrow.

Soon I began to wonder if I understood what tomorrow meant because the fights didn't stop and things were never better. One night Dad hit Mom so hard he broke her nose and for a lot of tomorrows Mom's eyes were black and blue and her nose and face were swollen to the point she almost didn't look like Mom any more.

One of the last nights we were together as a family, I couldn't stand hearing Mom's screams and crying any more. I figured I'd just stand up to my dad and say, "Dad, don't hit on Mom anymore."

My heart raced and my legs trembled, but I made my way through the dark hall to the living room where I saw Mom in a corner and Dad was just beating on any part of her his hands could find.

I froze.

How could I stand up to my dad?

He was like a giant, and when he was in a rage the way he was that night, he frightened me.

"Stop! Thomas can see what you're doing. Stop it!"

Words I didn't understand came out of my father's twisted lips. I got the meaning, and I turned and ran to my bedroom, buried myself underneath the covers and cried myself to sleep.

I cried because I hadn't been able to stop my dad.

I cried because my mom was still hurting.

I cried because I was too little to do anything else.

I loved my dad, and when I grew up, I wanted to be a man, just like he was.

Only I didn't like how he had treated my mom.

Guilt over not being able to protect my mom became a pretty constant companion for me.

Now, every night before I went to sleep, I checked all the doors and windows where Mom would be sleeping so that I could protect her in the only way I know how. I had never been able to protect her from my dad's hands, but I was six now and plenty big for my size.

Anyone who wanted to hurt my mom was going to have to go through me.

My dad had taught me well. No, actually my dad didn't teach me anything. He showed me. If I wanted anything in this world, I would have to get it for myself. Everyone was fair game, boy or girl, big or small; if anyone attacked me, I would use my hands to protect myself.

❧

My favorite times with Mom and Grandma were in the evenings and on the weekends. Those were the golden hours when I didn't have to worry about school and the kids who didn't understand me. I tried to be their friends. I tried talking to them. But when things didn't go my way, I'd feel the rage just build up inside of me and eventually my fists would fly.

As a result, when the weekends came along, I didn't have a lot of kids I could go to, knock on the door and ask if they could come out and play.

Mostly, I played alone.

So when Mom would say, "Come on Thomas, let's go gathering!" I'd hop to it.

I'd meet Mom and Grandma in the driveway where they would get in the front seat of the white four-door Honda Civic and I'd hop up on the hood of the car because we weren't going very far.

Our neighborhood was still so new, and houses were going up like beach umbrellas. Throughout the day the sounds of hammering, sawing, and other construction noises rang through the air. But by about five o'clock, all the workers had gone home, leaving skeletons of wood and fiberboard in their wake.

On the ground lay dozens and dozens of plastic and glass bottles and aluminum soda cans.

To us, this meant money.

I'd hop off the hood of the car, grab the trash bag Grandma handed me through the window and run and pick up all the bottles and cans at the site. Then I'd run back to the car, hand Grandma the bag and hop back up on the hood of the car for Mom to drive to the next site.

At first this activity was a lot of fun for me. I never got in trouble doing it, and it was fun being outside with Mom and Grandma going from house to house picking up the beverage bottles and cans. Then once a week we would take the bags to the recycling center and the man would pour the contents of our bags into a bin, weigh it, and calculate how much our stuff was worth and he'd give Mom some money for it. This she carefully put away in her purse.

On Sundays Papa would come along with us. One of their favorite activities was to drive over to any new housing development to go and look at the new houses. We'd drive along the roads of the fancy neighborhoods.

"Oh my," said Grandma. "How many bedrooms do you think that place has?"

"I'd say eight or ten," answered Papa.

"And at least four bathrooms," said Mom.

"That's a lot of bathrooms."

"That's a lot of bathrooms to clean."

Each house we would look at, it was the same thing. At first it seemed like fun, driving through the rich neighborhoods, imagining what it would be like to live in one of those mansions. But after doing it several weekends in a row, I started to get tired of it.

"Why do we keep looking at houses of rich people?" I asked.

"It's fun, Thomas. Wouldn't you like to live in one of those houses?"

That got me thinking and I promised myself that when I grew up, I was going to get one of those fancy new houses for my mom. She worked so hard and if anyone deserved to live in a house like that, it was Mom.

෯෧෧

Because Mom worked every day, and Grandma was usually home after lunchtime, I knew that if I was having a bad day at school, all I had to do was pick a fight with someone to be sent home.

For most kids at the school, being sent home was pretty serious.

For me, it was such a relief because I didn't get why the kids at school didn't understand that I only wanted to be their friend.

I wanted to play with them. Most of the time.

I did know that once I got the ball, though, I didn't ever want to give it back. It was like it was a prize and once I got a hold of it, I would hang onto it for dear life.

And that's what got me into trouble.

At lunch recess we were playing tetherball. I waited in line, dancing up and down; waiting to take my turn and finally when I got to play, my opponent was one of the bigger boys in my class. I was not going to let him beat me. The instant my hands got control of the tetherball, I hit it in such a way that it would swing up high over David's head, way out of reach of his hands, even when he jumped.

Smack!

Smack!

Smack!

Each time the yellow ball came around I put all my weight and effort into hitting the ball higher and faster. In no time I had wrapped the ball around the pole.

I'd won!

I loved the feeling of winning.

I looked around, expecting all the kids to be amazed at my achievement. They would certainly want to be friends with the best tetherball player in the class.

No one else on the playground looked as if they felt like celebrating.

"Who's next?" I tossed the ball back and forth between my hands, challenging the boys in my class. Maybe Kevin, he was almost as big as I was.

"You can't play anymore. You hit the ball too hard."

"No, that's not how we play the game."

"Well, we're changing the rules."

"No!" I could hear my voice getting louder. "Whoever wins plays the next kid. I won. I get to play the next kid."

What were they thinking anyway?

That wasn't how the game was played.

Why were they changing the rules on me?

I started to argue, but that old familiar feeling of rage built up inside of me.

Then David stepped up to me and grabbed the ball out of my hands saying, "Go away. No one wants to play with you."

That was it. I felt a hot lava river rush up into my head.

I slugged him in the back, right between the shoulder blades and he fell to the ground. David flipped over, ready for me as I jumped on top of him and we began wrestling and hitting each other.

"That's enough!"

"Cut it out, you two!"

Mr. Watson, who had been keeping an eye on my behavior, and the playground monitor pulled the two of us apart.

"Thomas, to the office," commanded the principal.

CHAPTER 3

I Want My DADDY!

Why was I in trouble?

"But they weren't playing fair!"

My protest fell on deaf ears. My shoulder was gripped in an iron grasp and I was led to the office.

This time, Mr. Watson made me wait outside his office while he called my grandmother.

I heard his voice, raised and angry. Usually, he seemed just resigned when he called home for someone to pick me up from school, but this time was different.

And the thing that made me so mad was that I wasn't the problem.

The kids out on the playground changed the rules just to keep me from playing.

How was that fair?

This time something else occurred to me. Why wasn't anyone else ever brought to the principal's office? Why was I the only one who got brought in? It felt like I was the only one getting into trouble and the other kids got off scot-free.

It sure smacked of favoritism.

When Grandma walked into the office a couple minutes later, the principal gestured for her to go into his office. She avoided looking at me as she went into Mr. Watson's office.

"Stay there," he said to me with a finger pointing back at the bench I'd just vacated.

This was new.

Usually I got to go in and listen to what he had to tell Grandma.

I sat back down and fumed again at the injustice of today's incident. Pretty soon I heard raised voices through the door.

"He needs help!"

"I know he needs help. Call in a school psychologist!"

"This isn't our problem. He's got ADHD or something. You figure it out. Take him to a doctor. Put him on some kind of medication."

"I expected that you would want to help him."

"We don't have time or money to get a school psychologist to come here and evaluate him."

And on it went. The volume of the conversation went down so I couldn't hear any more of what Mr. Watson had to say. I just sat on the bench not sure what I should feel like. This time things seemed serious. I wasn't going to be able to give Grandma my puppy-dog face and have it blow over by bedtime.

When Grandma came out of the office, her face was flushed and her lips were pressed together in a thin line.

She didn't even say goodbye to the office staff who knew her by name. They watched us wordlessly as she grabbed my hand and stalked out of the office.

We marched home and as we were crossing the street she burst out, "What would you think if you came home from school and saw me beating on Papa?"

Her question shocked me into silence.

Today I wasn't going to talk my way out of being sent to my room. No sweet smile and endearing voice was going to get Grandma to let me out early.

Today was definitely different.

When Grandma pointed to my bedroom, her face was very stern.

Yep, I was really in trouble this time.

But the image of Grandma beating on Papa disturbed me.

Ever since Mom and I had moved into Grandma and Papa's house, I'd been loved and hugged and cherished. Sure, I got in trouble, but the violence I'd witnessed when Mom and Dad were together didn't seem to have a place in our house.

Grandma beating up on Papa?

I couldn't conceive of it.

The question brought me back to my problem.

Why did I beat up on kids?

All that day, I lay on my bed listening to the sounds of kids across the street at school. I could hear the buses and cars queuing up to pick up students after the final bell. Once school was over, other kids in the neighborhood would go over to the school yard and play basketball or tetherball if they had their own balls.

The silence in my room seemed so loud.

Being sent to my room alone was about the worst punishment in the world. I hated being cooped up in my room, not able to be with people, not able to play with anyone. Being alone made me want to crawl out of my skin.

Why did Grandma think I had a problem? I was the MAN of the house. I needed to be able to protect myself and Mom. . . And I'd learned from my dad how to be a man . . . you use your fists.

When Mom came home, I heard the murmur of female voices as Grandma told Mom what had happened that day.

"Again?" I could hear the frustration in Mom's raised voice. She came to the door of my room, looked at me for a long moment and said, "Thomas, what am I going to do with you?"

I didn't think she needed to do anything but what she was doing. In my mind, she was a great mom. But I could see that she was waiting for an answer. I just shrugged my shoulders.

"Let's call your dad and see what he has to say. Wait here until I talk to him first." I could hear her talk to him on the phone, saying, "I don't know why he's like that at school. He never gets in trouble at home!" She paused to listen, then burst out, "I don't know. That's your child."

Dad didn't play a big role in my life, until Mom felt like she just couldn't handle me. By the time I was in first grade, Dad was back from Germany and living in North Carolina, making it easier for her to get in touch with him. That's when she would pick up the phone and call Dad.

My memories of him were hazy; mostly he was just a voice on the phone saying, "You don't let someone put their hands on you, Son. You have a right to stick up for yourself. To protect yourself."

I never told Mom what he said, because I knew it wasn't the message she really wanted him giving me. I also didn't tell her that I played the role of victim, telling Dad that someone else was trying to hurt me.

What I did like was having his support, telling me it was OK to stick up for myself.

Mom didn't like me fighting. She and Grandma both would tell me that words don't hurt. That I should never use my fists to fight back when all someone did was use words.

But they were both wrong. Words hurt a lot.

Having Dad's support even if we couldn't live together as a family was one thing that felt good in my life. Man, this guy used to box around the world. If he says it's OK to use my fists, then it must have been OK.

Once I got off the phone, Mom said, "Thomas, you're grounded for two weeks."

"That's forever!"

"You have to learn to stop fighting at school."

That old rage started inside of me and I said the only thing I knew would really hurt her as much as I was hurting right now.

"You want to ground me? Fine. I'll ask Dad if I can go live with him."

Mom's face told me all I needed to know. I'd hurt her as badly as I'd ever hurt her. She just turned her back on me and left the room.

I lay on the bed and tears pricked my eyes.

I could hear the kids playing in the neighborhood. A lot of them had their dads there playing with them, I could hear their deeper voices coaching their sons how to hit the ball, or how to stand for a free-throw.

Who was I?

What was I?

Was I human?

Was I adopted?

Was I really Mom's child?

Mom, Grandma, and Papa loved me, consoled me, and comforted me, but I didn't fit in with them.

I didn't fit in anywhere.

 measure

Once my two weeks of being grounded were up I headed down the street to Nathan's house. Nathan was probably the one kid at school who I could call any kind of a friend. I made sure I didn't pick on him at school because I didn't want to lose that friendship.

It's not because Nathan was the coolest kid in school, but because Nathan's dad was always around and I wanted some of that. Nathan and his dad were Clyde Drexler fans and talked constantly about the Portland Trail Blazers, so I became a fan as well just so that I could talk basketball with them.

When they would go and shoot hoops at the schoolyard, I would go over and shoot hoops too.

"Here, Thomas, hold the ball like this, and then as you shoot it move your fingers like this." I was infatuated with the bond Nathan and his dad had, and this was as close as I could get to having a similar relationship.

"Ok, boys, you want the other guy to go this way, so that you can go this way," and Nathan's dad would show us how to dribble, feint, and fake each other out. He sure knew a lot about basketball.

Every chance I got, I would run down to Nathan's house and knock on the door and his mom would come to the door.

"Hey, is Nathan here? Can he come out and play?"

Most of the time I wanted Nathan and his dad to come out and play, but just playing with Nathan was fine too.

Then there would be the times she would say, "Sorry, Thomas. He's not here right now. He's out with his dad."

I would walk home, dejected, wondering, what does it feel like to have a dad who's around all the time?

∽᎒᎒᎒∾

A few weeks later Mom came up behind me and hugged me, then held out tickets in front of me. "How would you like to go to an Oakland A's game?"

"Would I?" Was she kidding?

"We collected enough cans and bottles that I was able to get us a couple of tickets!"

Finally. I was going to get to do something my friends got to do with their dads. Go to an Oakland A's game. Wow! I could hardly believe it.

Getting ready for the game was like preparing for a red carpet event. We shopped for a new shirt and sweater because it was going to be cold, new jeans and brand new white sneakers for me. On the way to the game, we stopped by a barber shop where I went in and had my hair cut. Ever since being called "Brillo pad" at school, Mom and Grandma had tried to find a place to have my hair cut. Papa's barber didn't do any better with my hair than anyone else had, so Mom kept looking until she found this barber shop.

Mom always waited outside while I got my hair cut, and I finally figured out it was because she was the only white person in the shop. The guy cutting my hair said she probably didn't want to enter the "man cave" but I was pretty sure she was uncomfortable for other reasons.

Tonight, though, it didn't matter. We were going to a professional baseball game.

It seemed like it took us forever to get there, but once I saw the stadium from the freeway, it took us no time to park and enter the stadium.

It was bigger than anything I had ever imagined! A lot bigger than it looked on television. I held Mom's hand, squeezing it so tight so that she wouldn't be scared.

The game, the lights, the music, all made me grin like a crazed sports fan, which I was. The whole time I sat watching the game I wondered what it would feel like to be out on the field playing ball in front of thousands of people.

Man, that was some kind of attention!

Throughout the entire game, I was overwhelmed by the lights, the sounds, the intense green of the field, the cacophony of organ music, shouts, songs, and cheers. Mom bought me a hot dog which I devoured and an icy Coke which I slurped.

Everything was so intensely real.

I cheered and clapped.

Then I pretended that I was the one everyone was cheering for.

This was what I wanted.

On the schoolyard, I just wanted people to notice how good I was at playing ball. What did I have to do to change how people responded to me? The men in uniform on the field were the best athletes, and people paid good money to watch them play. They rooted for their team, for their favorite players.

How could I get some of that?

If only I could play on that field one day. I really, really wanted a stadium of people cheering for me.

All too soon the game was over and I realized it was dark. As we exited the stadium, I sensed that Mom was a little nervous. The parking lot looked really dark after the bright lights inside the stadium. After a moment of hesitation, Mom walked over to a group of police officers and said, "Who is going to walk a lady and her boy to her car?"

We got escorted to our car and safely locked in before the officer returned to the stadium. Part of me was irritated that she had asked for help, because I knew it was my job to protect her, but the other part of me was glad because I felt some of Mom's nervousness and fear.

All during the long ride home the sounds of the crowd, the excitement of the music, the intensity of the color of the grass under the night lights of the ballpark continued to thrill me.

Now that I had been to a professional ballgame, I began to picture myself in front of a crowd, on television. From that point forward, every basket I shot, every baseball I hit, I pictured myself as the best athlete on the field.

That night at the Oakland A's game was the birth of my dream. The seed had been planted in my brain that I wanted to be a professional athlete. Just as other kids said they wanted to be a dancer, or a writer, or a doctor, I knew that being an athlete was most definitely in my future.

⁂

As wonderful as the Oakland A's game had been, it only took me a short time before I was in trouble again at school.

"Thomas, what did we talk about this morning? You promised me that you wouldn't pick a fight!"

Mom was right. I promised her every morning that I wouldn't pick a fight, but I just couldn't help myself. It was the only way I got attention.

Professional ball players get plenty of attention.

That's what I wanted. I got plenty of attention when I pushed to be in the front of the line in class, or spoke up in class without raising my hand, but it just didn't get me the results I wanted.

I got attention for being the best at everything on the playground, but that confused me because while I was the best, no one seemed to want to play with me, not even Nathan.

That night after I went to bed, I heard Mom and Grandma talking. "You know, Mom, I wonder if he just needs to be around his dad."

I'd used that threat several times on Mom, saying that I would just go and live with Dad any time she punished me.

Each time I did it I knew it hurt her, but I began to wonder what life would be like if I lived with my dad.

CHAPTER 4

Wishes Do Come True

I have read stories about the kid who found a lamp, rubbed it, and out popped a genie who gave him three wishes. Other stories tell of fairy godmothers, or gnomes who give you what you want in return for a favor. I didn't find a lamp, don't have a fairy godmother, and would punch the lights out of a gnome.

But I still got my wish.

Just about the instant school was out for the summer, I would board a plane from Sacramento, California that would take me from my mom's loving but frustrated care right into the arms of my father in Fayetteville, North Carolina.

Dad.

A man I had only the vaguest memories of. Most of them were made-up from watching the kids in my neighborhood interact with their dads.

From what I could tell, dads played catch with their sons, took them to ball games, taught them how to wash and polish a car.

I also recalled some of the bad parts too, but they appeared in my thoughts like so many pieces of a fragmented mirror.

My last couple of weeks of school had flown by. I knew I would soon be living my dream life with my dad. After my last big dust-up at school Mom finally agreed that living with my dad might be a good idea.

I was later to learn that I shouldn't threaten my mom with words because she would say, "You go ahead and do that."

That last time I had threatened to go and live with my dad, Mom said, "Fine. As soon as school's over, you can live with your father and see how you like it."

To me, that wasn't really a threat. I looked forward to learning how to be a man and hanging out with my dad.

I was going to fight, spit, and burp like a real man.

We were going to play ball.

Eat pizza in front of the television.

Go to ballgames.

Together.

Being with my dad was my ultimate goal, to be able to experience what I watched other kids doing with their dads.

"I'm going to live with my dad. I'm going to grow up and be a man!" This thought, running through my head, got me through the last weeks of school.

As a gesture of both contrition and gratitude, I embraced the opportunity to make my mom a gift. It seemed like a good way to smooth things over because I could tell how upset she was about me choosing to live with my dad.

My Mother's Day gift to Mom was a little coupon book. Each page was a coupon that she had to rip out and once it was used she couldn't use it again. There were coupons for car washes, foot massages, making breakfast, cleaning up my room, cleaning out her car. The other gift we made was a recipe of my favorite meal of eggs and toast where she would hard boil some eggs, pull out the yolk and use the whites of the egg. That tasted so good to me and was my favorite meal. At school I made a recipe of it and put it in a nice little frame that she could put it on the wall. Part of me was a little selfish in making that because I didn't want her to forget how to make my favorite meal while I was gone.

⚬ᎾᎾ⚬

Right before I got on the plane, Mom got down on her knees and looked me right in the eyes. "Thomas, remember our discussions?"

I nodded.

"While you're with your father, I expect you to act right. You don't act out in school. You don't disrupt class. Don't interrupt the teacher. You get along with the other students, you hear me?"

I nodded again. It was pretty much the same thing she had said to me every morning before school for the past two years and on the days I had misbehaved, she would come home looking tired and disappointed saying, "Didn't we have this discussion?"

Every single time I meant it when I promised I would behave, but this time she didn't have to worry. "I'll be with my dad. I won't act out."

Her eyes filled with tears as she gave me one last hug, holding me like she didn't want to let go.

"Thomas, just remember to think before you act. Promise me?"

"Sure, Mom." I was itching to get on the plane and go live with my dad. Why didn't she seem to understand that everything was going to be different now? I kept watching the door where I would board the plane, fearful that Mom might not let go of me in time to board.

A woman in uniform came up to us. "This must be Thomas." Mom spoke with her in low tones for a few seconds, then hugged me again.

Every time she wiped her eyes, more tears replaced the ones she had just removed.

For me, it was almost a relief to finally follow the flight attendant and walk down the long hallway to the plane. Once on board, she strapped me into my seat, then handed me an airplane wing pin that I proudly pinned to my shirt. "Now Thomas, once the plane lands you stay in your seat until I come to get you."

Alone in my seat, I tugged my seatbelt just a little tighter and put my arms up on the armrests on either side of me. I could hardly contain my excitement. The force of the take-off pressed me back into my seat, its power matching my anticipation of going to live my new life with my hero.

All promises made to Mom dimmed.

High above the earth, thoughts of Mom, Grandma, and Papa grew as distant as the tiny trees, houses, and cars below me.

I'd never been away from Mom before, but going on an airplane all by myself to see a man I hardly remembered was just about the most exciting thing I had ever done. It never occurred to me to miss my old life. I just knew I was going to be way too busy with my new life to even worry about it.

Mom probably thought this would be a one year trial to see how I liked living with my dad.

What I couldn't tell her was that I never intended to come back. I was finally getting the chance to live my dream, to live with my dad.

At that moment, the idea of returning to California did not exist.

From now on, it was going to be Dad and me.

Nothing could be more perfect than that.

ഛഉ ഉഛ

When I got off the plane, I'm not sure how, but I knew the man standing at the end of the ramp was my Dad. He had a brief conversation with the flight attendant who had accompanied me to the gate to meet him.

There he was.

My hero.

I watched his face as he spoke with the flight attendant, marveling at how one side of his face moved and was animated, while the other side seemed etched in stone. Mom and Grandma had talked about Dad having a minor stroke, something called Bell's palsy that had paralyzed half his face. I'd wondered what that might look like.

When he finally looked down at me, Dad's face broke out into a smile.

It looked like only half of him was happy to see me.

The other half was just neutral.

"Well, T. Let's go."

‿ৱৎ ৫ৱ‿

I arrived over the first weekend of the summer and the first thing Dad did to bolster up my self-confidence was present me with a key to the house. "Thomas, this key is your life line. Do you understand me? You keep it with you, always. Every day you make sure you have it with you, especially once school starts because I'm not going to be home when you get home from school. I want you to start practicing right now how to be responsible."

Me?

A key to the front door of Dad's house?

I'd never had the key to my house before. I walked around, strutting my stuff, wanting to impress someone.

When we got into the car I expected us to go right home to Dad's house, but he turned to me and said, "T., I promised this friend of mine we'd stop by."

"Sure, Dad." That was OK. I was here to be with my dad. If that meant we were going to go to someone's house, I was along for the ride.

I hung back when Dad introduced me to his friends, unexpectedly shy and uncertain. They put on a movie for me to watch while they sat in the den drinking beer and talking and laughing. At first I kept looking into the other room to see if we were leaving yet, but I could see Dad was looking very comfortable with his friends. I went back to the movie and waited.

Just as the movie finished Dad came in and said, "Let's go, T."

Cool. I suddenly realized that when Dad said T., he was talking to me. I'd never had a nickname before. At home, I was Thomas.

Dad and T.

I liked the sound of that.

Our next stop was the bowling alley. "Let's do a little bowling, T."

I wasn't sure if I should admit it, but there was no way I could hide the fact that I'd never bowled before. Dad said, "Don't worry, T. I'll show you how it's done."

After I got fitted for the rental bowling shoes, he said, "Go and find a ball that doesn't feel too heavy."

I walked away from my dad and looked at all the balls on the racks. Some were plain black, others were pretty colorful.

The first ball's weight surprised me and I almost dropped it onto my foot. I didn't want to appear to be a wimp, so I didn't pick the lightest ball there, but some of them were so heavy that the finger holes felt like they were going to cut my skin.

"Bring that here, T." Dad positioned me on the line, bending over me as he showed me how to hold the ball. That was exactly what I had come to live with my dad for.

He was teaching me something.

He placed my fingers in the ball and said, "Now, when you swing the ball forward, your hand needs to come out of the ball like a handshake, your thumb toward the ceiling."

The first time I let go of the ball it went straight across the lane, right into the gutter. In fact the first couple of times, my ball fell into the gutter. But I wasn't going to give up. A couple times my ball managed to make it all the way to the end of the lane and knock over some of the white pins at the end.

"Way to go, T!"

His praise made me smile.

Then Dad taught me the various boards, where to aim, how fast to throw the ball. If the pins were set up a certain way, I was to aim at a particular spot. If they were set up differently, then I had to change my approach. He demonstrated. I watched and learned.

By the time we were done bowling, my arm and fingers felt like they were about to fall off.

On the way home I fingered the key in my pocket as I watched the man who was my father drive the car. He didn't quite live up to my expectations. For one thing, he wasn't as big as I thought he was. He didn't walk around with his arm around my shoulders, not that I expected him to do this all the time, but we hadn't seen each other in years. I'd expected some show of affection.

Since my dad didn't really know me, he tried to play it off as a joke, asking what kind of food I liked to eat.

"Just about anything!"

Dad laughed at my reply, but it was the truth. When I was hungry, I just wanted something in my stomach. We stopped for hamburgers before heading home.

It was dark when we pulled into the driveway of the house.

"Get out your key."

I pulled out my shiny key, inserted it into the lock and opened the door to my new home. The first thing I heard was a monstrous barking and growling coming from the back of the house. "What was that?" I turned to go back out the front door.

Dad laughed, "That's just Cho-Cho."

What's a Cho-Cho?

"He's a Chow."

At my confused look he continued. "Don't be scared, T. It's just a dog. Cho-Cho is my dog, T."

I looked at Cho-Cho and he looked at me. Cho-Cho made it very clear he wasn't happy I was there.

Cho-Cho saw me as an interloper. It used to just be him and Dad. Now I was there and he didn't like it. I could see we both suffered from the 'only child' syndrome, only Cho-Cho didn't bother to hide his irritation at me being introduced to the family.

Dad taught me to watch his tail for signals about his state of mind. "Look at his tail, when it's up on his back, that means he's happy."

As Dad stroked Cho-Cho, his tail was curled up high over his back, the dog pushing harder into Dad's hands to get even closer to him. Then as I reached over to pet him, his tail dropped.

"See, now, he's a little irritated."

No kidding.

"It'll take a little time for you two to get used to one another."

Dad showed me to my bedroom, white walls, a bunk-bed with a futon below covered with black pillows and comforter.

"Just leave your stuff there. We'll watch a movie before bed." Dad put in a movie and we sat together on the white couch watching "Boyz 'n the Hood."

The entire time through that movie, I just knew my mom would ground me for a month if she knew I was watching this. I liked it because the kid from south-central Los Angeles goes to live with his dad, played by Laurence Fishburne. As a dad, he laid down the law, the rules of what life was going to be like living with him.

"Here's what you're going to do: Clean the bathroom, rake the leaves, do the dishes, do your homework, etc."

I thought I was just watching a movie with my dad, but as the movie went on, I realized that the man sitting in the couch next to me had no idea how to talk to me. He was using the movie to tell me what life was going to be like with him.

Once the movie ended I looked over at my dad.

Without meeting my eyes, he got up and said, "You have your own room, but you can sleep in my room tonight if you want."

Because Mom and I had shared a bedroom for as long as I could remember, this sounded like a great idea. Until Cho-Cho realized that he wasn't going to get Dad all to himself. He sat at the end of the bed, looked me in the eye, and barked.

"Cho-Cho, be quiet," Dad said.

Bark.

"Quiet!"

Bark, bark.

I didn't say anything. I didn't like the barking dog, but I didn't like Dad's raised voice either.

After a few moments, Dad threw back the covers on the bed, grabbed Cho-Cho by the collar and threw him out the back door. He came to bed, turned out the light and rolled over and immediately went to sleep.

In the dark I listened to his deep, rhythmic breathing, to Cho-Cho's barking at the back door, and wondered what my life was really going to be like living with Dad.

The next day, Dad brought Cho-Cho back inside the kitchen and made him his breakfast. He didn't talk so much as grunt or point. Dad showed me where the Captain Crunch was in the cabinet and I was pretty stoked about that. Back with Mom and my grandparents, they would only give me one or two servings of healthy cereal to eat, and as a growing boy, I always felt hungry.

I ate one bowlful of cereal. Then poured myself another, and Dad didn't say anything. To test things even further, I pulled over the sugar bowl and spooned several scoops of sugar onto my cereal.

Still no reaction.

This was going to be great.

Dad only drank coffee and watched Cho-Cho wolf down his breakfast. After breakfast, Dad showed me pretty much what I'd learned from the movie last night. How to make my bed, where the trash went, cleaning supplies to keep the kitchen and bathroom clean.

I wasn't sure exactly how much he expected me to do, but I noted everything and nodded to show I understood.

When lunchtime came Dad taught me to cook.

"T., how about nuking us some cheese sandwiches for lunch?"

Nuke? What was nuke? I looked back at my dad and lifted one shoulder to show my confusion.

"You don't know how to cook for yourself?"

"I can make cereal."

"No, T. A man's gotta know how to feed himself. Here, toss me that bread and cheese over there."

I picked up the loaf of Wonder-Bread and threw it at Dad who caught it with one hand. He held out his other hand and I tossed him the package of American cheese slices, then watched as he put two slices of bread on a plate, topped each one with a piece of cheese and put it inside the microwave. A few beeps and the microwave began whirring.

I'd never touched the microwave back in California. Every single need I had, Mom, Grandma, and Papa took care of it. I never had to touch a microwave before moving in with Dad.

It was beginning to dawn on me that they had taken such good care of me and I had taken it for granted.

Dad pulled the sandwiches out and I could see that the cheese was just melted on top of the bread. "Now, you do it." And he handed me a plate. Copying him exactly, I put two pieces of bread on the plate and added a slice of cheese on top of each, leaving my wrappers on the counter just as he had done.

"Put it on for fifteen seconds, and no longer, or you'll fry the bread." Now I knew that a microwave can not only 'nuke' things, but 'fry' them too.

As my lunch heated, Dad pointed at the wrappers I'd left on the counter. "I expect you to clean up after yourself."

His meaning clear, I picked up the wrappers and placed them in the trash can. When the microwave beeped, indicating that my lunch was done, I sat down in the kitchen, but Dad looked at me, frowned, then indicated that I was to follow him with his head.

We ate lunch on the couch in the living room in front of the television. I learned we would eat most of our meals on the couch.

Like men.

Watching HBO with its programs of cursing and nudity.

Dad's viewing choices were a big change from 20/20 that my grandparents always watched. I was also allowed to watch ABC Kid's Saturday Morning when Grandma and Papa worked around the house.

Back in Vacaville on Friday nights I watched "Step by Step" and "Family Matters", and "Home Improvements" . . . at Dad's we'd turn on the television and HBO was usually the first thing that came on and the language was the kind of thing that would have gotten my mouth washed out with soap at home.

This was everything I'd dreamed it would be.

ᗡᓍ ᓍᗡ

Monday morning dawned and I made breakfast by pouring cereal into two bowls, one for me and one for my father, and topping them with milk. I didn't realize my mistake until Dad made himself some coffee and pushed the second bowl of cereal over to me. Coffee was his breakfast. It didn't bother me, I was happy for a second bowl of cereal. As I crunched my way through the sugary crispness, Dad set down the ground rules. Or rather, more ground rules.

Yesterday morning he made sure I knew what was expected of me. My bed was already made when I went into my room because I decided to sleep alone last night. But this morning Dad paused by my room as he was leaving.

"Make your bed, Son." Dad had pointed at my unmade bed, a black bunk-bed/futon arrangement. Back home Grandma usually made sure my bed was made every day.

I pulled the covers up over the pillow.

"No! That is not how you make a bed." Dad showed me how to make military corners. They looked pretty good. I smiled up at him. Then he pulled them back out and said, "Now you do it."

It didn't make a lot of sense to me to make a bed and then just unmake it like he had done, but I matched my movements to what he had shown me. When I was done, I stood back expecting great praise.

He tilted his head as he carefully inspected my work, and then pointed to where I had just shoved the blankets together under the mattress. "See right here? That's not right. Take it out and do it again."

I made the bed three times before he was satisfied. Then he said, "OK, that's the only time I'm going to help you make your bed. Every morning I expect you to make your bed just like this. Can't have any slobs living in this house."

"OK, Dad." This was fine with me. Dad's bed was perfectly made, too. I'd peeked into his room just to see what his bedroom looked like, and the tightness of the blankets and sheets on his bed told me that he was telling the truth. No double standards. I could get used to that.

When I returned to the kitchen I noticed Dad was dressed in his military uniform and it was about five in the morning.

I rinsed the cereal bowls from breakfast and listened as Dad said, "While I'm at work, you don't open the front door. You can go outside in the back yard, but you stay in the yard. Don't talk to anyone. Don't leave the yard. You understand?" His orders marched into my head like soldiers.

"So you can't stay home then?" I hated sounding like a sissy boy, but I'd only had my dad for a day and a half, and now in the weak early light of Monday morning he was leaving me. Who was going to take care of me?

"No, T. I have PT this morning and then I got a whole day's work to get done. I'll see you tonight."

I nodded, but my heart dropped. I'd neglected to consider the fact that Dad would be working all day. Back home, Grandma or Papa were there to keep me company during the summer when Mom worked.

As Dad drove away, I looked around the house. It wasn't big, just three bedrooms and two bathrooms. Plenty of room for the two of us.

And then there was Cho-Cho.

The dog stared at me.

I stared back at him. I'd never had a dog before, and Cho-Cho's size intimidated me a little. But, he was a living, breathing being, and I seriously hated being alone.

"So Cho, what are we doin' today?"

Cho-Cho cocked his head as if to say, "Fool, what I do every day. Sleep." And he proceeded to do just that. He curled up in the living room and I sat there watching the clock as the seconds ticked by.

Dad had left me with a complete control of the remote for the television, so that's where I started. At Mom's, my television time was very restricted and I never played video games. I was always outside playing. But I could adapt. This was my new life with Dad. Having full permission to watch nudity on television and learn new cuss words was an entirely new world for me.

At lunchtime I 'nuked' myself a couple cheese sandwiches. Drank a glass of milk. And returned to the television. No one around to tell me what to do, I finally got tired of the nudity, violence and cuss words, and I turned on cartoons and watched the colorful images until I heard Dad's car pull into the driveway. By the time his key turned in the lock, I was waiting by the door for him.

Not once had I disobeyed him.

"How'd your day go, T.?"

I grinned at Dad. "Great! I made my lunch, just like you showed me."

Dad glanced in the kitchen, "And you left your wrappers and paper plate on the counter. Didn't I ask you to clean up after yourself?"

He wasn't angry, but I didn't even want him to be disappointed in me. I rushed over, picked up the offending pieces and threw them away.

Dad opened the refrigerator, pulled out a beer and handed it to me. "Open that for me, would you?"

I'd never touched a beer before in my life. But this is what Dad wanted me to do. It would be my job every day when he got home from work.

Then Dad pulled out a package of pork chops and started heating the skillet. As soon as the pan was hot, he used a fork to put the pink meat onto the hot surface of the pan, the meat searing as he did so.

Pork chops with rice and black-eyed peas.

After dinner, we sat in the living room where Dad skimmed channels on the television. "T, help me pull off my boots would you?"

"Sure, Dad." I loved saying that. I hopped off the couch and knelt in front of him, pulling the top boot lace to undo the bow. I loosened the first few holes of the lacing and tried to take his boot off, but it was still too securely fastened to his foot.

"Boy, stop being lazy and undo the whole boot! Do it right!"

Immediately, I did as he asked, loosening the laces all the way down. I didn't see why he wanted me to do that, I had my shoes so just the top two laces needed to be loosened before I kicked them off. But, I wanted to please my dad so bad that I did exactly as he directed.

"OK, now you can pull them off."

Now I had two jobs when Dad came home from work; crack open a beer and take off his boots.

∽ઉ૯ ૭૭∾

The days melded into one another.

It started with breakfast together, after I'd made my bed and picked up my clothes. Our quiet time together in the mornings made me believe that Dad and I were really bonding, even though we didn't have a whole lot to say to each other yet.

At one point Dad got me a bike so I could go outside for some exercise and at first I was pretty excited until he repeated his rule that I was to never leave the front door.

"You can ride your bike, but only in the back yard."

The back yard? Was he kidding? It was the size of a postage stamp.

Cho-Cho and I went out back after Dad left. "Well Cho-Cho, guess it's just you and me." By now, Cho-Cho followed me around. I was slightly more interesting than napping all day. I got on my bike and started to ride around the tiny back yard. After watching me a moment, Cho-Cho followed me, so the two of us, feeling neglected began to bond in that special way boys and dogs do.

Cho-Cho and I had conversations. I had no one else to talk to. I'd met no other kids yet and school hadn't started. Life with Dad was less exciting than I had imagined it would be. So Cho-Cho became my friend, like my brother. Circle after circle in the back yard, we traveled, each of us wondering where we were going.

In an odd way, I'd finally made my first friend.

※ ※

When Dad came home on Friday he said, "Pack a bag, Son. We're going to the country." I learned that really meant, "We're going to see your grandparents."

As I carried my bag to the car I learned something else about Dad. Every time we went somewhere in the car, Dad grabbed a washrag and covered up the handgun he pulled out from somewhere, and carried the gun by his side out to the car where he hid it.

I sat beside Dad in the front seat of his '85 pearl white Oldsmobile with the red rag top and buckled myself in. Going to the country sounded exciting after a week of endless boredom being home alone during the day.

"Where are we going?"

"My mama lives in Lakeview, South Carolina, just across the border in South Carolina."

"Where are we now?"

"We live in Fayetteville, North Carolina. Your grandma's place is about seventy-five miles away."

That didn't answer my question and like every little kid I asked over and over again, "Are we there yet? How much further?" I probably asked Dad every five minutes, "How much longer are we going to be?"

Most of the time, he's just say, "T. relax, we'll get there when we get there."

Dad got on I-95 heading south out of Fayetteville. Once outside the city limits the land looked distinctly different. There were fields and trees as far as my eyes could see, with an occasional barn or farmhouse breaking up the monotony.

For the most part, all I saw were trees.

Miles and miles of trees.

Dad turned on the radio, nice and loud and we grinned together. Everything Dad did, I did. He put his elbow out the window, so I tried to do the same thing, but I was too short to pull it off. It looked more like I was scratching my head with my elbow, so I settled for putting my elbow on the armrest on the door.

We listened to music as we drove, but we really didn't talk.

The only time Dad stopped was if I really had to use the restroom. For the most part, once we got in the car, we went from Point A to Point B with the precision of an engineer.

Periodically Dad picked up his car phone and dialed a number and from his side of the conversation I knew he was talking to one of his lady friends.

I didn't know anyone back in Vacaville who had a car phone. Something about the way Dad punched those phone buttons and put the phone up to his ear made me imagine the President when he traveled in Air Force One.

About the only time Dad said anything directly to me was to point out the sign that said we were leaving North Carolina and entering South Carolina. "We're just about there." And then he spoke again once we hit the Dillon Highway. "Only fifteen more minutes."

That was enough time to start getting a little nervous about meeting Dad's family. I wondered about my Grandma. I knew I must have met her when he and Mom were still together, but I had been very young then.

We pulled up in front of a house. The doors opened and people poured out of the house.

"Let's see you! Oh my, aren't you a big boy."

"Just the spittin' image of your dad."

"Come here and let your grandma look at you."

"This here's your cousin, Keith."

"This is your aunt, well not so much an aunt, but she's been a friend of the family so long, she's your aunt too!"

"Ray, he's just the spittin' image of you."

"That's what I just said!"

"We're just going to have to call you TR, aren't we?" The cacophony of voices peppered me with questions.

"How's your Mom?"

"Did you know you look just like your dad?"

They confused me because they were calling Dad 'Ray' and calling me TR. I remembered Mom calling Dad TR and I wasn't sure I wanted to be called that.

We climbed the steps into Grandma's double-wide with everyone moving in a gigantic mob. There were so many people I couldn't figure out who I was related to and who were friends and neighbors.

Where did I fit into this family?

For a boy who had spent a good part of his life living with three adults in a California suburb, it was culture shock. I had no idea I was related to this many people. As we entered the house I smelled some of the best smells in the world. Grandma and my aunts were in the kitchen stirring pots filled with fried chicken, gravy, mashed potatoes, collard greens, and much more. I didn't have to say much, everyone around me was doing plenty of talking. Someone said, "You kids go on outside and play now. We'll call when dinner's ready."

After being cooped up in Dad's house for the past week with no access to the outside world except his small back yard, I didn't need to be told twice. I followed the kids outside, some who were my cousins, and some who were kids of friends who were like family. We chased one another, playing tag, throwing sticks, and whooping it up in general.

Just being around kids was the best part for me. Some bigger, some smaller, we played tag, hide-and-seek, and pole-to-pole, a game they'd made up running from one light pole to the next in the street. Unlike at Dad's house, we played outside, in the street, in other people's yards.

Dad had grown up in Dillon, so he felt comfortable enough there to let me play out of sight of the house. In Dillon, everyone looked out for everyone else's kids.

I hadn't been around this many kids since I'd left school, but it was different here. Here, I belonged, even though I don't ever remember meeting any of them before.

We heard the call that dinner was ready and I raced back inside, my blood pumping, my heart racing, filled with the thrill of having some kids about my own age to play with.

My grandmother was an amazing cook. I ate more food than I remember eating in one sitting except maybe at Thanksgiving. Everything tasted so good after a steady diet of fried pork chops, rice, black-eyed peas, cheese sandwiches, and cereal.

The steady sound of voices talking over one another, the laughter, the overall feeling of being cocooned inside of love wrapped around me. This was what I'd come to live with my dad for.

We stayed for the weekend and I discovered that the meal Grandma had prepared wasn't something special in my honor. She cooked like that every day because the next day it all started all over again, more fried chicken, more collard greens, beans, rice, macaroni and cheese that didn't come from a box. By the time we got in the car for our return to Fayetteville, I was stuffed so full that I was almost uncomfortable.

"Well, did you have fun?"

"Yeah." I grinned up at my dad. I sure did. But once we got back to Dad's house and I got ready for bed, I realized that I'd missed having my own space, my own bed, my own TV. At Grandma's house I shared everything because people slept everywhere, and most of us kids either slept next to one another on a floor somewhere, or three to a bed.

I got into my bunk-bed and breathed in the silence of no one else in the room with me. I could sleep how I wanted. Watch what I wanted.

I was also happy in the realization that once we got home, I had my dad to myself again. But in a perverse kind of way, I missed the level of activity at my grandparents. I'd just come from a weekend with a house full of people back to where Dad and I were alone, except for Cho-Cho. It was hard for me to figure out exactly what I wanted. At Dad's house I had independence, but it came at the cost of being lonely.

CHAPTER 5

Doing What Dad Taught Me

Visits to Dillon took on a regularity I found comforting. Because I was the baby, everyone would comfort me and coddle me, and there was a part of me that liked that. But the really competitive part of me took some stage time too.

On one visit in particular the weather didn't cooperate. Rain and fog kept us kids inside and underfoot. Finally my cousins could tell that Grandma was getting a little exasperated and said, "Hey TR, let's go and watch TV or play video games or something now."

Grandma was a great believer in playing outside, but she was also a great believer in not having to clean up a bunch of mud every time we all came indoors. Time spent in front of the TV was rare at Grandma's, so to be allowed to play video games was a change.

My cousin and I took the controls and I discovered something about myself. I love playing video games, but I love winning even more. Every time my cousin would beat me at the game, I became more and more frustrated and angry. So much so that when Dad and I were driving home from that visit I said, "Dad, can I get that video game Keith and I were playing?"

"Why?"

"Because I want to practice before we go down there next time. I want to beat him the next time I play him." The only time I ever got to play that video game was when we visited together at Grandma's house. I wanted the chance to beat him.

"That's my boy," Dad laughed.

True to his word, Dad got me the video game and my lonely hours in the house while Dad was working took on a different purpose. Now, instead of trying to keep myself from dying of boredom, I played that video game from the time Dad left in the morning until the time he came home in the evening. I learned every nuance of the game, every possible way to get to the next level, how to stay alive even when things didn't look so good. At first Dad played the video game with me, but after a while, I was so good at playing, that he got frustrated and refused to play with me anymore. I guess Dad didn't like to lose either.

The next time Keith and I squared off in front of the TV set, I beat him over and over again.

My natural competitiveness became my constant companion. It joined me in everything I did. When we would race from the tree to the house, I ran as hard as I could. My uncles laughing and jeering at me, saying, "You can't run, Thomas! You're too white." I didn't care that I was only half-black in Dad's family; I only cared about beating my cousin. I didn't care that he was three years older and three inches taller. I would burst my heart and lungs in order to beat him in a race. I would jump over and over again just to touch the net of the basketball hoop that my cousin could touch without any effort. It wasn't in me to just accept that I couldn't do something.

Dad took great pride in my competitive spirit saying, "You're going to be some athlete one day, T."

❦

Second Grade started for me in the form of Mrs. Carter at 71st Elementary School of Cumberland County Schools in Fayetteville, North Carolina. Because my dad had instilled such a strong sense of responsibility about my key during the summer, it was second nature to me to check every morning that the key to the house was secured in my backpack. Because if I didn't have my key when I got off the bus, there was no one to let me into the house.

Mrs. Carter and I started off the year as usual. By this I mean I didn't see the point of going to school. I hated sitting inside on a hard chair at a desk all day, every day, just looking at that beautiful sunshine outside and there I was, stuck inside a dusty, smelly classroom.

It was only a matter of time before my true nature came out at school. I picked fights with kids who made fun of me.

I didn't have the problem of not having a dad now.

I had the problem of not having a mom.

Most of the kids in my school had moms. Not all of them had dads, so for me to have a dad and not a mom was a problem.

As usual, I took care of the problem with my fists.

Only I couldn't exactly get sent home from school at 71st Elementary because I had to take a bus to school and Dad was working. He made it very clear that I couldn't get suspended from school. So I rebelled in other ways.

Every week we were given spelling words that we were supposed to study for the test every Friday. After a couple of weeks of my spelling word list traveling to and from home and school in my backpack, it became evident that learning to spell via osmosis wasn't cutting it.

Dad started to spend Thursday nights quizzing me on my spelling words. Being that Thursday night was the first time I had even looked at the words, I didn't do so well. This made Dad mad, but didn't really bother me. Mom used to get mad at me for not doing my homework too. Her anger never motivated me to make a change.

Dad had a few tricks up his sleeve. He shocked me by just appearing in my classroom one day. He'd had enough. Phone calls from the principal did not make him a proud parent and rather than just accept it like my mom and grandparents back in California did, Dad took action to make sure I behaved. He figured someone wasn't telling the truth. In his mind he thought, "My son is telling me one thing and the school is telling me another." He was determined to get to the bottom of the problem.

I was certainly better behaved in school when he was there. If Dad saw me act up, he would wear me out when I got home. Also, when he was there I couldn't say, "The teacher was lying. I didn't do that."

I had made so many excuses to keep myself from getting into trouble that it was second nature. When Dad was in the classroom, I couldn't slant the story in my favor. His presence really cramped my style.

No one's dad ever sat in on the classroom. Moms were there just about every day, but never dads. I wasn't sure how to take this turn of events. Dad didn't join the classroom to help. He made it clear he was there to keep me in line. And the whole time Dad was there, I could feel his eyes burning a hole in my spine. I didn't dare look out the window, throw spitwads, talk out of turn, or sass Mrs. Carter.

Dad managed to do something Mom hadn't figured out how to do. He made me aware that I could get through a day of school without getting into trouble. Having him there was humiliating. I had a sense of pride in my dad being in school, but the main feeling was one of humiliation. It was like having the military police in the back of the classroom making sure I didn't mess up.

So now, the threat of Dad coming back to my classroom was enough, most of the time, to keep me from misbehaving.

But it didn't help that much with my spelling words.

സൈ ളൈ

That fall Dad started dating a woman whose son and I hung out when she and Dad would get together. One day, his dad came to pick him up because he played in a flag football league. I felt that sense of emptiness that I'd felt back home. I didn't love the game of football, but I hated that feeling of being alone and left out of anything.

As fall progressed, Dad asked me, "How would you like to play flag football?"

Would I? I played flag football on the playground every day, and if anything, I got in trouble because I didn't bother just pulling the flag off the kid, I just tackled them. Pulling a flag was for sissies. But it was something to do.

When Dad went to sign me up, he was told that it was too late for me to sign up and play with a team. The teams in the league started several weeks before and had already played a number of games.

This was something that Dad wasn't willing to let go. He knew how much being active meant to me, and once he made up his mind that I was going to play flag football on a league team, he wasn't going to take "no" for an answer.

Each day was a constant effort talking to another league, or talking to another school district, or rec center. Every single day, Dad did something to try to get me on a football team.

Soon I began to think that my dad was out of his mind. We'd been told "no" not just once, but dozens of times. But Dad didn't give up. His relentless effort to get this accomplished showed me that when you want something you never stop.

I began to worry that there were league rules or team rules that were keeping me from playing. Or maybe the teams just didn't want me. My own feelings of concern didn't affect my dad one bit.

He never quit trying to get me on a football team.

Eventually, one team said, "Fine, Thomas can play."

And I did get to play.

One game.

We started looking for a team late in the season. That in addition to the amount of time it took to finally find a team that would let me play meant we were at the end of the season.

But I got to play football.

And I got to play because Dad taught me that you can't quit just because you got denied the first time, or even the second time. Or even if you're told it's against the rules, or "we can't do it."

Dad taught me that even when it looks impossible, things are still possible.

Now I had something to share with my dad. I enjoyed the game of football and because he had spent so much time getting me on that team it had to be important to him too.

Once the game was over, my dad was absolutely beaming as I walked toward him. It was almost as if he were seeing me for the very first time. After that, we would watch football from time to time on TV.

I really didn't have a clue about the rules, the terminology, or the guidelines. What did make an impact on me, though, was that people took time out of their day to watch men play football.

I had played football, and moms and dads from all over the city had taken time out of their day to watch us play football.

I wanted to have that happen again.

CHAPTER 6

Be Careful What You Wish For

I travelled to Fayetteville to learn to be a man. And Dad was teaching me all kinds of things. When I said goodbye to Mom in June, I didn't really think that I would miss her, mainly because I was so excited to live with Dad.

I had been of the mind, "Bye, Mom. I'll see you." When I left I didn't think once about looking back.

I had lived for such a long time with a gaping hole in my life, that of missing my dad. When I set out to live with him that was the only thing on my mind.

As second grade marched on, I began to realize that my dreams of living with Dad were much different than reality. It was very different from the life I had led in Vacaville with Mom, Grandma and Papa. With Dad I spent a good part of each afternoon after school completely alone, basically under house arrest because Dad didn't want me going outside.

I would watch other kids with their mom's cooking dinner and loving on them and kissing on them. When I got home I'd get tough love from a man I didn't really know. At school kids would tease me asking, "Where's your mom? Why don't we ever see your mom? You don't have a mother, do you?" I was getting teased in North Carolina the same way I got teased back home in California when people would say, "That's your mom? She's white. You're not white."

Now, I was getting the exact same treatment only on the opposite end of the pendulum. "Is that your dad? Really? He's black. You're not black."

My sense of identity was as fractured as my family life.

‿◌ ◌‿

My dad had a lot of girlfriends. When we would go places, to parties or to homes of Dad's friends, often kids asked, "Is that your mom?" And then when the next girlfriend attended the next event, it would be the same thing, "Is that your mom?"

Their questions infuriated me.

The women in Dad's life seemed to be stepping into the shoes of my mom and I didn't want that.

I had a mom.

She just didn't live in North Carolina. I knew that if I still lived with her, she'd be kissing on me and hugging on me. I hadn't realized what I would miss until I no longer had it.

As a result, I never let any of Dad's girlfriends try to be my mother. I never let them get that close to me. Every time one of them would talk sweet words to me or try to hug me, I would pull away and close myself off emotionally. To me, each new attempt was just another one of Dad's women and she didn't mean anything to me. If anything, all the women in Dad's life just confused me.

I wanted to ask him, "Hey dad, it was Monique a month ago, Nicole just last week, and now we're on to Devonne. What's going on?" Only I didn't have the courage to challenge Dad that way.

What I did know was that I had to stand in line for Dad's attention.

One of Dad's girlfriends tried really hard to buy my affection. She took me to the mall where she asked, "Hey, T, would you like to get an earring?"

That was a loaded question.

I knew my mother wouldn't approve of me getting an earring. It never occurred to me to ask Dad.

I said, "Sure."

Dad's latest girlfriend signed the paperwork just as if she were my mom, handed over her charge card, and when we left I had a new hole in my ear and a brand new earring.

Dad was furious. More because he didn't want to deal with my mom's disapproval than because he didn't like it.

What I learned from that experience was that people will do just about anything to buy my affection and loyalty. What Dad's girlfriend didn't understand was that I saw things as Dad and me against the world. She wasn't with us, so in my mind we were against her.

The jealously I felt toward the women in dad's life stemmed from my intense need to be important to Dad. The women in his life took up his time, his money, and his emotions.

That left me with nothing.

If we ever went anywhere in a car, I had to sit in the back seat and I hated that. My place was in the front seat next to Dad. Every time I found myself in the back seat, I would just glare at the back of the woman's head, thinking really evil thoughts. I wanted to drive those women out of Dad's life. If they were to ask me how they looked I would say, "You're fat. You need to lose weight. And you smell funny." I did everything I could possibly do, including being rude. They just laughed it off as if I were being cute.

I was anything but cute. I hated them.

The first time Dad had one of his girlfriends over for the night, I heard them making noise in the bedroom. Because Dad and I were very open about the way we lived together, I just opened the door and walked into his bedroom. "Dad, what are you doing?" I was making up for lost time, and the idea of having to share my precious time with my dad with one of his lady friends didn't make sense to me. To me it was no different than hearing him tinkering out in the garage, and I'd open the door and say, "Dad, what are you doing?"

So I didn't understand when the woman screamed at me to get out, diving under the covers. Dad shouted at me to close the door and to not come in without knocking. I sat outside the bedroom door, still listening to their whispers, fierce and furious, trying to figure out what was going on behind that closed door.

How was I going to be just like my dad if he didn't let me in on everything he was doing?

Pretty soon, I heard them showering and I knew they would be coming out of the bedroom, so I made myself scarce by heading back to my room and playing video games. When Dad came to the door I was totally preoccupied.

"Thomas, we're going out for a bit. Would you like to go get something to eat with us?"

I was burning up with so much anger, frustration, and jealousy that I ignored both of them. Dad waited for a minute, and I could see them exchanging looks, eyebrows raised, shoulders shrugging.

"OK, T, that's the way you want it. That's just fine. You stay here and don't open the front door."

I nodded, refusing to look at him. I never looked at the lady behind him I'd already seen plenty more of her than I had ever wanted to see.

They paused in the doorway for another uncomfortable moment, and then Dad said, "All right, T. We'll be back."

"Sure, Dad." My thumbs showed more emotion than my face did as they manipulated the video game controls.

Once I heard the front door close and lock, I threw down the video control and hopped off my bed. At my dad's bedroom doorway, I hesitated. I'd never been restricted from Dad's room before, so now I wanted to know why. I explored the room and saw a box of something called Trojans on the nightstand. This must be a manly thing to have. I took a few packets out and sounded out the word c-o-n-d-o-m. I put one in my backpack so I could show the kids at school what a man I was becoming. I only took one because I didn't want Dad to know I'd taken something from him. Later that week when I got in trouble at school for proudly showing the condom around, he asked, "Where did you get that?"

There was no way I was going to admit to Dad I'd stolen it from him. "It was just around. I found it."

Dad was satisfied with my answer.

༺༄ ༄༻

In addition to women, Dad really enjoyed drinking. Any chance I got, when there wasn't a woman staying over at the house, I was next to Dad. Some nights he'd call me into his bedroom and just let me lay there with him in the darkness while he slept. Sometimes he would drink too much and pass out on his bed for a long time on the weekends and I would just lay there with him. I checked occasionally to make sure he was still breathing. I don't know where I got the idea that he could die, but a new worry erupted that if he died I would have no one to take care of me.

One Saturday he had been drinking a lot and he called me inside from where I'd been playing outside.

"Aw, Dad. It's still light out." But he insisted and I went inside where he ended up going to sleep. As I played my video game I would glance over at him from time to time, just checking on him. I didn't know if I should throw away all the beer containers that were sitting around or not. I didn't know if I should try to wake him or not. I did know that him sleeping that hard so early in the day wasn't normal and it gave me a funny feeling in the pit of my stomach.

One day, Dad and his current girlfriend had had an argument and she left the house with screams and slamming doors.

As usual, I just focused on the video game in front of me. I could hear him breathing, so I knew he was still alive.

An hour or so after she left, Dad called me into the bedroom. "Hey Thomas. I need you to call my lady-friend."

I stood at the door of his bedroom just looking at him. "I don't want to."

"Call her!"

"No."

"Thomas, call her. Tell her I have a gun in my hand and you think I shot myself."

One thing my dad had been teaching me since I arrived to live with him was that I should never lie. I hadn't made a habit of lying before I moved in with my dad, but he'd made sure I knew better than to lie. I might get in more trouble for telling the truth, but I just didn't lie, so Dad's request really conflicted me.

"Come on Thomas. Call her! Tell her I'm on the bed with a gun in my hand and I'm not moving!" He was almost sobbing at this point.

I wanted to help Dad, but I knew this was wrong. Besides, he didn't have a gun in his hand and he wasn't bleeding.

"Thomas, you can have whatever you want, just call her for me!"

All right, maybe my principles weren't quite that strong. I wanted a go-cart I'd seen down the street. I'd been after him for months to get it for me.

"What do I get if I call her?"

"Anything! Anything you want!"

"How about that go-cart I showed you?"

"Anything, Thomas. Just call her for me!"

He was crying. Begging me. Pleading with me.

Alcohol really made my dad do crazy things.

"I want that go-cart down the street."

"Ok. Fine. Done deal. Just call her."

I called.

"I don't believe you," she screamed and slammed the phone down.

"She won't believe me, Dad."

But she must have believed something because within a few minutes there was a knock on the door. When I peeked through the front room curtain I saw police, reporters, and a camera crew set up in front.

"Open the door, Son."

"No way, Dad." And I moved away from the door.

Dad answered the door and I listened to him play the whole situation off as a lie.

"Oh, I fell asleep with my gun in my hand. I was cleaning it. My son must have thought I shot myself. I'm fine. See?" Dad held his hands up and turned around for everyone in our front yard to see that he was fine.

I watched in disbelief. So this is what a woman could do to a man. There he was lying to the police, and I was in the lie too. He convinced me to lie for him, so now we were both lying to the police and everyone.

The only consolation was that we were lying together.

That was when I began learning the hierarchy of my principles. Being a man like Dad took on more importance than not lying.

The same lady friend came back. She couldn't resist Dad's money and for some reason she really got under his skin. By then, whenever she came over, Dad would let me go play out in the front yard so that I didn't come knocking on the bedroom door to see what they were up to.

One day as I was playing, I heard her screaming. She barreled out of the house, jumped into her car, and frantically started it still wearing next to nothing. Then she backed out of the driveway. I had to jump out of the way because I could tell she didn't see me. With a screech of the brakes and a grinding of the gears from reverse to drive, she tore off down the street. Just as she pulled away from the house Dad came running out, shirtless, shoeless, holding his pants up with one hand. He stood in the middle of the street shouting at her to come back.

Visions of my mom screaming came back to me, so I figured some of the same thing had been going on in the house. Still in the middle of the street, Dad pulled a gun out of his pants.

I thought, oh God, he's going to shoot at that woman.

Dad drew his gun, aimed it the receding car and held his position for a very long time, both of us watching the car getting smaller and smaller as it moved away from us down the street.

He didn't shoot.

He walked back to the house, and then as if he just remembered me, he turned and looked at me, his eyes unfocused and glittering, "Thomas, we have to go. It's time to go in the house."

I wondered if any of the neighbors might call the police because he'd drawn his gun, but I let him get us both inside the house in case anything happened. I didn't dare say a word once we were in the house. I sat on the white couch and just watched as Dad went about hiding his gun. After wrapping the gun in a washcloth he hid it under the cushion of the couch. Then he seated himself on top of it. I sat at one end of the couch and he sat on the other end, directly on top of a gun wrapped in a washcloth and we both waited. He didn't say a single word to me.

It was a given that the police were coming. Even I knew you didn't go waving a gun in public and not have the police notified.

What if he went to jail? The worst part of my concern is that I was afraid for myself. If Dad went to jail, where would I live? Would I have to live in South Carolina with Dad's family? Would I go back to Mom in California? And if that happened, how could I possibly tell her what just happened?

The police came and talked to my dad for a very long time. They ended up not taking him away to jail. I don't know if it was because he didn't shoot the gun or if it was because he had a license for the gun.

That night as I went to sleep I thought I'd live with my dad so I could learn to play catch and go to ball games, and do father-son things together.

Instead, I slowly learned that my dad was a crazy man who had a lot of guns, liked drinking, and women.

CHAPTER 7

I Want To Go Home

E verywhere we went I was exposed to alcohol. At Dad's friends' houses, everyone was drinking. Every day Dad expected me to open a beer for him the minute he got home, and he would yell at me if I didn't do it right away.

No one else in the second grade knew how to crack open a beer. I even brought an empty beer can to school just to show the kids I wasn't telling tall tales. I did get in trouble then. Dad spanked me.

But that was the pattern of my time with my dad as he showed me how to be a man. I accompanied him on all of his drinking, womanizing, and gambling escapades.

The funny thing about all of it was that he would tell me the whole time to not do what he was doing.

Who was he kidding?

I'd come to live with him to learn all the secrets about being a man, and I wasn't wasting a moment.

We'd go to different events and parties every single weekend we didn't go to South Carolina. At the different houses, some of Dad's friends had kids about my age and we'd be put in a back room to watch television or play video games. The only constant was that Dad almost always took me with him. He didn't trust babysitters, so along I went.

Being put in a back room with the other kids never kept me satisfied for long. I was still curious about what Dad was doing and by then I had some pretty serious concerns about him. It was just the two of us, so I had to do everything in my power to make sure that nothing happened to him.

Back in the kids' room I'd worry. Was he out there getting so drunk that somebody was going to beat him up? Was he running his mouth so loud that he's going to get into a fight and maybe have someone shoot him or kill him?

None of the other kids in my school ever admitted to having problems like that with their dads.

As soon as I heard a loud commotion in the room where all the guys were gathered, I would go out and say, "Hey Dad, I'm ready to go home now."

Usually I had a bad feeling. I didn't feel safe and I felt I had to get Dad out of there. I just knew something bad was going to happen and I wanted to get out before it did.

"Come on, Dad. I want to go home. It's late." It would be about one or two in the morning and I struggled to stay awake to keep Dad safe.

Sometimes Dad would say, "OK, Thomas. We'll leave in a little bit." Then he'd shoo me away. "Go on, now. Get back to your video games until I come and get you."

I'd obey and go back to the room.

Most of the time when I tried to get Dad to leave the alcohol, the women, or the gambling, he wouldn't even look up at me. It was as if I didn't even exist for him. His world revolved around those three things and at times I was so desolate that I would turn around and wipe away tears of anger, sadness, and frustration.

After several times of trying to get Dad to leave, I'd finally fall asleep, cuddled among all the guests' jackets on the bed. Eventually I knew it didn't make any difference if I asked him to go home. It was just easier to go to sleep than to have him ignore or reject me again.

When he was finally done, he'd pick me up, sling me over his shoulder and carry me to the car. By the time I got to the car, I was awake and terrified again, because I knew now that we had another problem. He'd been drinking for hours and hours and now he was going to drive us home. I felt that I had to stay awake to make sure we didn't crash into a tree.

✺ ✺

Dad's parties were always drinking parties. It was never, "Hey, come on over for some burgers, maybe a couple of beers, and have a laugh." For me, staying awake became a necessity because I never knew when we left if we were really going home or to some other party. I didn't want to fall asleep and then wake up not knowing where I was. I also worried that someone would follow us home, pop out of the bushes and hurt my dad.

The parties were strictly adult parties where there was cursing, foul language, and loud sexy music. I knew the lyrics to more sex songs than I did Sesame Street songs because that's what I was exposed to.

Dad was a sergeant in the military, and at home I was raised like a military kid should be. I made my bed. Got up early. Cut the grass. Shined Dad's shoes.

At the parties, Dad exposed me to a very different life.

Gambling.

Always gambling.

Dad's friends behaved like a huge fraternity. They got together every weekend and their favorite activity in addition to drinking was gambling.

I learned to play dice and craps before I could spell words. I learned how to add up fast.

I learned what snake eyes meant.

I know what box cars and 3s and 6s and 7s and all those different gambling terms were because I was right there.

I wanted to be just like my dad. He was my hero.

So, I watched him play dice.

Cards.

Dominoes.

Dad and I would play dominoes for hours. I was only in the second grade, but I learned how to make a good bid and how I could lose my money making a bad bid.

One night I went with him to the barracks and I watched him play dice. We got there about nine or ten o'clock in the evening and didn't leave until it was two or three o'clock in the morning. On the way home, Dad pulled over and pulled out all the money. He had eight hundred dollars in ones, fives, tens, twenties, and a single one-hundred dollar bill that he let me hold and look at. "Look, Son! Look at how much I made tonight!" I'd seen him play and knew that it started at a one dollar bet, then a three dollar bet, moving to five dollar bets, and then ten or twenty dollar bets.

The sight of all that money only increased my desire to be just like my dad. I learned my lessons well. From that point on, I was right there on the linoleum floor of the barracks on one knee, just like my dad was sitting. I watched him throw the two dice up against the wall, calling out different numbers.

I learned how to gamble. And I was good.

Dad used to have a big old gallon Alhambra jug and he put all his change in there. Every night he'd reach into his pockets and I'd hear the faint jingle of the change he would have in his pockets. He'd pull it all out and drop it into the jug.

I learned to shoot or pitch nickels; throwing the nickels to see who could get as close as possible to the wall. Whoever did, won the pot.

I took this nice new talent with me to school.

I couldn't spell to save my life, but on the playground, I knew how to hustle. I'd hustle for lunch money, for snacks, for toys. It was never more than a couple of dollars, but I was doing that because that's what my dad taught me, and anything he taught me stuck like glue.

Then I'd get caught at school. The school would call Dad. He would punish me and send me to my room for doing the very things I'd been learning by watching him.

I was so desperate to learn about being a man that no amount of punishment made me learn my lesson.

꧁꧂

I'd hear stories about people drinking and shootings. People talked and with everything I heard I felt like I was becoming a man of the world. They weren't your regular bedtime stories. Someone always got hurt, and I figured it was just a matter of time before it was going to be my dad.

One time Dad left me home to go out and party.

I was home by myself.

I didn't have a babysitter.

I was not at someone's house.

He was there when I fell asleep, when I woke up I discovered he had gone out. I was afraid to be alone at night. I kept telling myself to just fall asleep, the sooner I fell asleep, the sooner the night alone would be over. Cho-Cho was with me and I was glad of the company.

But the fear I had was that something would happen to my father and I wouldn't know who to call to take care of me.

The next day, I found out that my dad had gone to a function, a club or something. There was a fight and someone had hit him, punched him. Dad returned to the house to get his gun and go back to take care of the guy. But as he went by my room and saw me there, asleep, he told me that was the only reason he didn't go back.

✵ ✵

In the early days of living with my dad there was only one time that I disobeyed him. I'd gotten into an altercation with a kid named Brian. Nothing really major, but it had been bad enough that my friend Neil called and said, "Hey, I heard you and Brian went at it today."

I explained the story to Neil and started talking about Brian's family, bad-mouthing him, same as I'd heard my dad talk about people. I felt like I was a pretty tough guy hanging around grown folks. I found myself speaking like them, talking like them. I'm big. I'm bad. I'm tough. Nobody can do anything to me.

Neil said, "Hey, come on over and we'll hang out." Dad wasn't home, so I left the house. I wasn't supposed to leave, but I left anyway because I was going to hang out with Neil. We were going to play video games and hang out.

I walked through the door, saw Neil, then I saw Brian, the kid I'd been badmouthing and there was one more kid behind the door. I froze.

They set me up.

They beat me up right there in the house, kicking me in the face and punching me in the stomach.

Finally they stopped.

I ran home.

I was bleeding and my pride was wounded.

There I was, a big tough guy in second grade, and I discovered that I wasn't as tough as I thought.

All the way home I plotted how I was going to get them back.

But they outnumbered me.

I needed something.

My dad had always told me, "Son, when you fight, you don't fight to fight fair, you fight to win the battle."

When I got home, I tore through the house looking for my dad's gun.

That would settle things once and for all.

It's what Dad would do.

Part of me didn't want to find the gun, but at the very least I wanted to go back down there and wave Dad's gun around to scare them.

But I couldn't find the gun.

So I couldn't go back and wave a gun in their faces. I don't know if I was pleased or not. I certainly didn't want Dad to come home and find out I'd taken his gun out of the house.

By the time Dad got home, I'd concocted a story about playing football explaining away my injuries. Being very protective of me, Dad would have lost his mind if he found out that I'd gotten beat up.

⋰⊛ ⊛⋱

Dad kept probably half a dozen guns in his house. Some were handguns, like the one he hid from the police under the couch cushion. Other guns looked like the kind you would see in a mobster movie. The house I lived in with dad had guns hiding in a lot of places, but because he changed the hiding places, I wasn't able to find a gun to go and avenge myself.

Dad always said, "T, you keep quiet about these guns, you hear?"

I nodded my head vigorously. There might have been something illegal about some of the guns he had. But Dad had grown up in South Carolina where guns were a way of life.

I asked, "Dad, can I have a BB gun?"

He looked at me for a long time, then said, "No."

Just that.

No.

No explanation or reason. Just no.

I wondered why. He had guns.

On a visit to Grandma's house down in South Carolina, I stayed for a long weekend so that I could be around kids my own age. I liked it because I had freedom there. Dad was comfortable enough to let me stay by myself.

Dad's stepfather noticed my interest in the guns around and said, "TR, you want a BB gun?"

Dad had so many guns, and I really wanted a gun of my own. Having a gun was one way a man showed the world he was a man. It was also a way of spending time outside shooting at cans, bottles, and targets there in the country. I had set up a campaign where every waking hour I talked about getting my very own BB gun.

It worked.

One morning, Dad's stepfather drove me to the Walmart store and got me a BB gun of my very own. I learned to use it while we were in South Carolina. And when Dad found out about it, he was pretty upset with me, but because family had given it to me, he couldn't take it away.

After that incident with Neil and Brian, guns made me feel a little sick to my stomach and I was afraid of using the BB gun on my own. Being around guns confused me. In South Carolina, guns were just part of living in the country. But in Fayetteville, it was different.

Dad's irresponsible behavior with guns highlighted for me that guns were to be concealed and only used to threaten people.

That was wrong and I knew it. I knew Dad could get in trouble for the way he used his guns and I didn't want that either.

He was my dad and I loved him.

I also knew that looking for the gun to wave in the faces of the guys who beat me up was wrong. But it hadn't stopped me from trying.

I'd like to think that I would have just used the gun to scare them.

I'd like to think nothing else would have happened.

⊷⊙⊙⊷

Knowing comes from training and being taught.

I'd come to live with Dad to learn to be a man, but the dads back in California hadn't behaved the way Dad did.

My expectations of living with Dad had been high. But as the year groaned on, more and more I wondered. I thought that the prize about having a dad was a special relationship between just the two of us.

When I left California, I'd imagined an advertisement for a dad rather like an apartment: For Sale: One Dad. Must play catch once a week. Must watch kid-appropriate movies, eat pizza, and spill popcorn on the couch every Saturday night.

This was a classic case of bait and switch. I'd come out to live with dad to learn how to be a man. He hadn't taught me anything I could take back home to Mom or to my friends at school. Most of what I'd learned from Dad got me into nothing but trouble.

Dad manipulated people by buying them things. Including me. It was like he was buying their love or something by spending time, effort, and money on them. I saw no benefit in having them in our lives, they just wanted him for his money, women especially. But even his friends wanted him around because Dad was definitely the life of the party. But everyone who wanted dad around had a "what's in it for me" mentality. Dad could never see the lack of true attachment or genuine organic caring.

I was seven and eight years old the year I lived with Dad. I saw how his friends treated him.

One night as I lay on the top bunk of my bed I knew this was not the life for me. I had plenty of *things* in my life with Dad.

What I *didn't* have was that close, loving relationship that Mom and her parents had shown me.

Life with Dad confused me. I saw him using condoms, but when I took one to school, I got in trouble. I learned to gamble and gamble well at his knee, but when I took my new-found skills to school, I got in trouble. Same with the beer can.

Why were adults allowed to behave that way and kids weren't?

I felt miserable living with Dad.

I had to tell him that I wanted to go back to live with Mom. It took me some time to work up the courage. He would be hurt and might even try to buy my affection by promising me things if I stayed. But nothing he could buy with his gambling winnings would replace how much I missed Mom.

Be careful what you wish for, because when it comes true, you might regret it. I had gotten my wish to live with Dad, but as in so many stories and fairy tales, my wish didn't quite live up to my expectations.

Finally I blurted it out.

"Dad, I want to go home."

I could see in his face how much that hurt him.

"But you are home, T, home with me."

"No, Dad. I want to go home to Mom." What I couldn't tell him was that what he had wasn't a home. It was just a place with four walls and a roof where two guys live.

I knew what to expect at home with Mom. With her, I could talk things out, figure things out.

Dad didn't have time to be a father. He didn't understand me and I had to compete for every single second of his time.

I was miserable without Mom.

It was time to go home.

CHAPTER 8

Home

Mom met me at the airport, her arms around me like she never wanted to let go. It had been a whole year since I'd seen her, felt her hug. My face snuggled into her shoulder. I could have stayed there forever. Finally she released me, stood up with her hand still on my shoulder as if reassuring herself I was really there. After our emotional reunion she said, "You remember that I've been seeing Ron, right?"

I nodded. I'd actually met Ron just before I left California a year ago to go live with Dad. Part of me was happy that Mom would be seeing someone, and I was glad that it was still Ron. Mom and Ron picked up my bags and we went out into the California sunshine to our new home together. As soon as I smelled the air, I knew I was back home. Nothing smells quite like California.

My only concern about moving in with Ron was that he might try to be my dad.

I had a dad. And while he might not be the perfect dad, he was mine. Just like when I lived with my dad, I wanted all his lady friends to know I had a mom.

One of each was enough for me.

But I had nothing to worry about. Ron was friendly, nice, and easy to be around. He joked with me, made my mom smile a lot, and was willing to go outside and play ball with me. Not once did he try to be a substitute dad to me.

One thing I had learned while living with my dad was to be polite. The first time I wanted to get a drink of milk I looked at Ron, "Can I go to the refrigerator?" I felt like a guest.

"Thomas, this is our house. You don't have to ask permission to open the refrigerator." That settled that problem. At home I knew my place and it was very comfortable.

It was only when we went out in public that some of my former insecurities returned because now I knew I looked black. Mom and Ron were both totally white. When I was with Dad I was "too white" and now living with Mom and Ron, I once again feared I was "too black."

Strangely enough, there was never a conversation about me being biracial. I could never bring myself to ask Mom about it. In my own mind, I began to run the stories of me possibly being adopted again. I felt like I just didn't fit in. More importantly, I didn't want to know the truth. Was I adopted? You just don't ask the question if you don't want to know the answer.

I loved Mom so much I didn't think I could stand it if it turned out she wasn't my real biological mother.

⋰⊚ ⊚⋱

Soon after I got home we went to watch Ron play softball. He was semi-pro and as soon as I saw him on the field I recognized his capabilities. He was a high-effort, high intensity player; never taking his eyes off the ball, constantly talking on the field. He'd be telling his teammates where the ball was going to go, how far it would probably go, and who to watch out for.

This was knowledge of the game I simply had to get. As I watched him play I wondered, how does he know where the ball's going to go? Why is he talking so much? What's he saying? One thing I knew, his chatter on the field wasn't annoying from some kind of know-it-all who has a lot of knowledge but can't play the game.

Ron knew the game.

The other thing I noticed as we watched the game is that when Ron spoke, his teammates listened to him, respected him. That was something I wanted. I wanted people to look up to me, to listen to me, to think that whatever I had to say was important enough to pay attention to.

Ron and I would stay up late watching baseball games on television and that's where we really bonded. He'd teach me the rules of the game, the secrets that aren't found in any rule-book anywhere. He knew exactly where the pitcher should pitch the ball for each batter, what pitch to throw, and he could predict where the ball was going to be hit. How did he know so much?

Ron was like a baseball encyclopedia, and I absorbed as much of that information as I could. Any time Ron would turn on the television and I'd hear the roar of the baseball crowds, I'd go over and stand there watching the television. It only took a few times for Ron to pat the couch beside him for me to feel comfortable just sitting down next to him and I'd start asking questions. Ron was happy to tell me anything I wanted to know.

Ron didn't passively watch a ballgame on television. He commentated all the way through the game. He had a conversation with the television.

Turn two.

Curve ball.

Low and outside.

He'd predict what pitch was going to come next, what pitch was coming up. It didn't take long for me to realize he wasn't just repeating what the commentators were saying. He taught me about foul lines and the foul poles. How many players on a baseball team? What was a double play? When do you bunt? What's a sacrifice fly?

This was a whole new language I was learning and every time we sat down, I learned more and more about how to be a better baseball player. With that kind of interaction, Ron gave me permission to think, talking as if we were actually playing in a game. I learned that there were strategies behind every pitch, every swing, every bunt. Every single time the ball was in play, there was a strategy, and a reason for everything that happens on a ball field.

Ron gave me a voice by challenging me with questions, "Thomas, what would you throw here?" Or, "Runner on first and second, do you bunt? If so, what side of the diamond do you bunt to? Third base? First base?"

For the first time in my life, I felt like my voice, my opinion in something mattered. I could make a call. Even if it was wrong, Ron never chastised me by saying, "That's not what you do!"

Instead, he educated me by asking, "Why would you have thrown that pitch?" Or, "Why would you hit the ball to that part of the field?" And then he would walk me through it. "Let's think about this. Strategically, if you have a left-handed pitcher he's going to throw the ball from the mound on the right hand side. So you're going to want to bunt the ball away from the direction the pitcher's momentum is taking him." Ron was a brilliant educator because I always felt engaged and wanted to learn more. He never made me feel bad about myself so that I shut down. He challenged me to think, to reason through a situation.

From Ron, I learned critical thinking skills. He talked to me as a grown man, not as a third-grader. As a result my thinking with regard to baseball really evolved. Some people may say he was teaching me life skills, but all I knew was that a grown man, with an interest in sports, took time out of his life to educate me about it.

We would play catch outside. I was the only third-grader in my school who knew how to throw a curve ball. My favorite activities were when we actually attended professional ball games at Candlestick Park. There we would watch the San Francisco Giants play. That's when I finally felt a little like I was experiencing something my friends with dads experienced.

෨෨෧ ෨෧෨

Ron and Mom lived on Westwood Court, which was on the other side of town from where we had lived with Grandma and Papa. One of the things I loved about being back with Mom was that she didn't keep me confined to the back yard. But because this was a new neighborhood, I really didn't have any friends yet. Night after night I'd go outside with my baseball bat and just practice swinging. I was sure that once they could see what a powerful batter I was, they'd invite me to play ball with them. Evening after evening, I'd go out and swing my bat, but no one ever invited me to play. Usually Ron came out and we'd play catch for a while.

"Don't you want to play with any of the kids in the neighborhood?" he asked me one day.

"Well, yeah, but no one ever asks me to." Even to my own ears my words sounded like a pity party. I looked for approval, and being invited to play was peer approval. The year I lived with Dad, every time I went into a room where he was he would shoo me away. Now living back in California, I feared being rejected by the kids I wanted to play with.

"Thomas, if you want to play, just walk down there and say you want to play."

I looked at Ron and he held my gaze. This was a guy who knew what he was talking about when it came to baseball, and I'd seen the way people respected him and looked up to him. Finally I nodded my head. "OK, I'll do it." I walked past Ron, gave him a high-five and set off to make some friends.

From that day on, I spent hours and hours playing sports with the neighborhood kids.

They were a lot better than I was at everything.

I'd thought all this time that I was the best at any sport around, and here in the neighborhood and at the park I discovered that these kids had been playing sports since they could crawl. Sure, I had the raw ability, but they had the knowledge, skills, and understanding of the rules that could defeat my talent every time. Some of them were bigger kids, in fifth and sixth grade, but even some of the second and third graders knew more about the sports than I did.

The person who knows more and is smarter about the game will beat a person who is naturally better every time.

It all comes down to strategy.

My natural competitive drive kicked in and I learned as fast as I could about everything. They knew the terminology, they knew the lingo, and even called out various plays. I didn't ask them to teach me, I learned by listening.

I didn't have to be the loudest kid on the playground or on the court. In order to learn what they were talking about, I had to just shut up and listen.

Whatever I didn't understand, I'd go home and ask Ron because to ask my friends would make me feel inferior. My ego couldn't tolerate that.

Ron was safe. He wouldn't yell at me. He wouldn't belittle me. Whatever I wanted to know and understand he would explain to me until I understood. With the kids I played with, I was much more private.

At the park, we played without too many rules. No one called fouls. No penalties.

When I played too rough I lost out on opportunities. Kids would head to the park without inviting me to join them.

They also excluded me from a lot of weekend parties and activities because I was like a big Labrador puppy who didn't know how to play gently with a miniature poodle.

On the weekends Ron and I watched football. My friend, Jack, down the street and his dad were Philadelphia fans. They loved the Eagles and they loved the Phillies. Their connection to a team was really amazing to me. What did it feel like to have a team because that's your father's team and your grandfather's team? Other friends in the neighborhood were fans of the San Francisco teams, the Giants and the 49ers. On Sunday everyone would watch football and then once the game was over, we'd all meet outside and emulate what happened during the game.

We pretended that we were actual players, playing in Candlestick Park. Jack was always the quarterback and I was always the wide receiver, and we reenacted what we had seen on television right there in his front yard. He would alternate being Steve Young and Joe Montana, I would be Jerry Rice. From the first time we played football in his front yard, I had the dynamic I was looking for.

I belonged to something bigger than myself.

At this moment I gave myself permission to dream.

To dream about being something more than I was. I pretended this would be us in high school and the papers would write about us. Jack as the quarterback, I'd be the running back, cheerleaders leading cheers chanting our names, and fans cheering us on.

The more I thought about it, the more I knew this was what I wanted.

CHAPTER 9

When's Recess?

I began to feel as if I lived two lives. Playing sports made me feel part of something and I had friends. When I wasn't playing sports, I found myself getting into trouble just as I had done my entire life. I liked being tough, but I was no longer the biggest kid on the block.

Most of the time when I would try to bully kids into doing things the way I wanted them to, they would end up attacking me and things always turned into a wrestling match. I always lost in wrestling. Whenever I was at someone else's house and a fight would break out, the kid's mom or dad would come out and send me home, standing there until I left.

Making fun of other people came easy to me, but when people made fun of me, I hated it. I couldn't take it.

Mom said, "If you can't take it, don't dish it out."

That never stopped me. I thought I could take it, I was a tough guy. I usually said something that would hurt the other person more. I was king of "one-up". It disguised my pain.

After being sent home I'd walk into the house, dejected. Sometimes Ron was there when I came home. "What happened?"

I usually shrugged my shoulders or say, "I don't know." A few times I managed to tell him as much of the truth about the situation as I could handle. I never told him just how much I would make fun of other kids, or that I would try to beat them up if they made fun of me.

Ron would listen and one time he said, "You have to learn to be the kind of person people want to be around."

Yeah? How do you do that?

I never understood the social rules where everyone got along. I never had it in for any of the kids; I didn't bully anyone just for the fun of bullying them. I just wanted them to do things my way, and if they didn't want to, then I felt I had the right to exert my influence until they did.

⋆⋆⋆

One kid in particular made my neighborhood feel more comfortable. Jason lived directly across the street from us. His mother was white and his father was black, giving us an instant kinship, even though he was more than twice my age. Jason became a mentor for me. He was older than all the kids in the neighborhood. Anytime I wanted to talk to someone closer in age, I knew I could ask Jason because he wouldn't make fun of me.

One night I took the trash out after dinner and Jason was pulling their car out of the driveway. He'd just shown me his learner's permit the day before, and I was appropriately impressed. He and his dad were going out driving, and as he paused in his back-up turn, he gestured me over.

"Yeah?" It was neat that an older kid would actually talk to me.

"If you ever want to shoot hoops on my court, just come on over. You don't even need to ask."

"Thanks!" Wow, someone who didn't mind if I came over. That was a really good feeling. From that point on I would go over to Jason's house to play basketball, sometimes alone, and sometimes Jason would come out and shoot baskets with me. It felt a little like having an older brother.

I wanted to be just like Jason. He would tease me, roughhouse with me, and just treat me like a younger brother. At fifteen, Jason was much bigger and stronger than I was. In a way, by wrestling with me, Jason was toughening me up, making me ready for the rough and tumble times at the playground and at school. But later when I played sports, he taught me how to hold my own. I could never beat Jason, but I kept going back.

In order to continue to improve, I had to always look for a better competitor. Jason helped me to hone my skills. I hated to lose. Every time I wrestled Jason I knew I was going to get beat, but I also knew I was going to learn something new and become better at it.

෯ⓔ ⓔ෯

As summer drew to a close, I realized that I didn't really know what to expect in terms of school. Here I was, going into third grade, my fourth school in four years. You'd think I would be an expert at making new friends.

I worked really hard to get attention, but always the wrong kind.

I interrupted in class.

I picked on some kids who I knew no one else liked just to get approval. They ended up crying, reporting me to the teacher, and I ended up in the principal's office.

At recess, I was always picked last for games. How could they not see that I was the best player out there? What was wrong with them? That made me try even harder and more aggressively than before just to prove how good a player I was.

Games of touch football always turned into a game of tackle because I wanted to show my dominance over the other kids. I hated to lose, so if my team was losing, I would just take the game to another level in order to win. It wasn't enough to just play by the rules.

The pros don't do two-hand touch.

The pros don't play with flags.

I didn't want to be a sissy kid playing with flags; that was a fake game. Now tackling. That's a real man's game, just the way you watch on television. You are not down until you are tackled. There is no gray area in getting tackled. In two hand touch, kids would just say, "No, you didn't touch me, Thomas."

Oh yeah? Well, let me show you next time. I won't touch you. I'll tackle you. That way, no one can say you're not tackled.

I wanted to be a winner. I wanted people to point me out to others and say, "That kid, Thomas, he's a real winner, a real champ." That was my goal.

Nothing worked.

I would get in trouble because someone always got hurt. Someone would tell and a yard supervisor would come over, grab me, and I would be escorted to sit on a bench and have to watch for the rest of recess all the other kids having a good time. All this did was make me angrier and my mission became one of just showing them the next time how wrong they were.

Day in and day out I found myself sitting on that bench, thinking, why are you picking on me? What did I do? Why did I get in trouble? I found myself watching other kids enjoy something I couldn't enjoy. And to make matters worse, the longer I had to sit on that bench, the more pent-up energy would build up in me that I couldn't burn off on the playground. I often came in very angry after recess. Sometimes I would take someone else's seat, just so that I would be noticed. Other times I would make sure I spoke louder, faster, and before anyone else, just so my teacher would notice me.

At some point in the afternoon I would be asked to leave the classroom for misbehaving.

My recess problems became classroom problems because when I didn't get noticed on the playground, then I longed for it even more in the classroom.

But my teacher didn't understand.

Neither did my principal.

To them, I was just a problem.

Alamo Elementary had two separate playgrounds. Because I was in third grade, we played on the kindergarten through third grade playground, while the older kids played on the playground for grades four through six. After enough timeouts on the bench and letters home to my mother, she and the principal agreed to let me play in the big kids' playground to see how I did.

Their rules were different and I didn't like it because it wasn't my playground anymore. The kids on this playground were bigger, faster and stronger than I was. I still didn't get picked first whenever the sports games were going. What I really didn't like was that I couldn't jump to the front of the line for tetherball or wall ball as I had on the other playground. The bigger kids forced me to wait my turn. Or worse, they would all take cuts in front of me when I tried to be nice and just wait my turn.

I felt that I just couldn't get a break.

♦♦♦

Eventually my behavior at school got so bad that Mom and my teacher devised a plan. They created a journal out of a notebook. Each day I gave it to my teacher who would write messages to my mom. At home, I had to turn it in to Mom to have her sign that she'd read what was in it.

I hated it.

Mom was adamant. "Thomas, this is the only way we know to help you hold yourself accountable for your actions."

What were they talking about? What was accountable? All I ever wanted was to have friends and play.

They insisted.

Mom said, "This way I will know how well you're doing in school before your report card comes."

Before this new accountability step, Mom would ask, "How was school today?"

"Fine."

"Any problems?"

"No."

But the truth of the matter was, there were problems. I wasn't stupid, that wasn't the problem with me. I just wanted attention from my teacher. If talking loudly or out of turn didn't get her attention, then I'd start talking to someone else in the class. I craved interaction with other people.

Instead, whenever I talked out of turn or distracted a classmate, I would be removed from the class. This never made sense to me because the longer I was out of the classroom, the more instruction I missed. There would be assignments I never got, or key words that would be on upcoming tests that meant absolutely nothing to me.

How could I be responsible for knowing something I never was told I was supposed to know?

It never occurred to me to go to my teacher either during recess or after class to see what I missed that day. At the age of eight, my goal at recess was to be the first outside and at the end of school to race out of the building as if it were on fire.

I always rode home with the same group of kids. I never wanted to be left behind, so I made sure I was at the bike rack before anyone else. As we rode our bikes home from school, I felt a part of something.

Once school was over, I totally forgot about it.

Until Mom asked to see my journal.

"Thomas got sent out of class twice today."

"Thomas had to miss."

"Had to move Thomas away from the other kids."

"Had to send Thomas to the principal's office."

"Thomas got in trouble during recess."

Every single little issue at school that day was written down in the journal. It became the very bane of my existence.

I hated that thing.

Every time Mom would open it and see how I had managed to get into trouble, I would be grounded. I couldn't play ball. No television. Extra chores. Confined to my bedroom. Sometimes I had to write out my punishment.

Write five hundred times, "I will not fight."

Out came the yellow pad of paper with twenty-five lines to a page and I would start, I, I, I, I, I...all the way down to the bottom of the page.

Next word, will, will, will, will...all the way down to the bottom of the page.

I continued to do it this way, it seemed easier to me. As punishment, it didn't teach me to not to fight. I never connected all those words. I just wrote a bunch of symbols. What it did do was keep me from being able to go outside and play.

I hated sitting still.

That was pure punishment for me.

Before school the next day, Mom signed and dated my journal. I handed it in to my teacher. Never did my teacher ever write that I had done something well.

It was always, *always* bad.

It felt like I was in jail or something and my mom and my teacher were my parole officers.

CHAPTER 10

Please God, Let Me Be . . .

B y the end of third grade, I pretty much hated everything about school. But I knew I couldn't keep going that way. For an eight-year-old, I had a pretty good understanding of what it meant to be an adult.

Of all my role models, Ron was the one I looked up to the most. He was a semi-pro baseball player and well respected in the community. My dad was in the military and he spent his time and money gambling, drinking, and carousing. My mom worked so hard every single day cleaning houses for other people that she came home exhausted. My teacher had no time or patience with me.

I wanted to be like Ron.

The only bright spot for me was the news I had made All-Stars in Little League baseball. Being in All-Stars meant people noticed me, noticed my abilities. I had been chosen to be on the team. They *chose* me!

I was finally good enough for somebody to notice that I was worth something. Baseball became my life-line. I went out for it because a bunch of other kids were doing it. I figured if they were trying out and I was the best one on the playground, why not?

Ron coached me and he told me just before I went for the draft at the park. He said, "Thomas, the first time you get a chance to throw a baseball, throw it as far as you can. Don't even try to hit the person with the glove. Don't throw it accurately. Throw it as far as you can to show off your potential, your arm strength."

For me, this was another competition and I was determined to be the first one drafted. I'd watched the NFL draft where it said, "the first pick of the NFL draft is . . ." I imagined them calling my name.

To be drafted meant I had been chosen.

I was accepted.

I was wanted.

I'd set my goal to be picked, and sure enough, here was this kid, this *nobody* from Vacaville, California and they were calling my name.

During baseball, both practice and at the games, I did not misbehave. This was a place where I was totally comfortable. I understood what was expected of me.

I knew how to keep my mouth shut and I wanted to pay attention.

I was getting recognition so I didn't have to act out to get it.

This was baseball and I was good at it.

Yeah, pretty soon, people were going to know about Thomas Williams.

During All Stars I gained everything I was looking for, recognition, acceptance, appreciation, camaraderie, teammates, the game itself, and the events.

It was during that first All Stars season that I learned about making friends. My teammates became my brothers.

I never did anything to hurt any one of them. None of them came from my school so my bad reputation didn't follow me on the field.

I was actually good at something.

Something real.

For some strange reason, that made me wonder about my future. What was I going to do when I grew up?

While I didn't have a lot of religious background, I'd been taught to say my nightly prayers. The idea of a higher power appealed to me and it gave me someone to talk to who didn't actually ever talk back to me, which at this time in my life was a good thing, because usually anything I ever heard from people was how bad I was messing things up with my life.

I was happy to talk to God, this higher power because one thing that was really on my mind was that my mom needed protecting.

What if something happened to me when I wasn't around?

This nighttime ritual between me and God was a good moment for me. It gave me the opportunity to ask God to look over my mom, watch her, protect her, and then I would feel comfortable enough to go to sleep.

Then I'd add in everything else, "God bless my mom. God bless my dad. Please protect my grandparents and all my loved ones."

In my mind, this was a pretty good idea, because what if I did "die before I wake?" Who would look out for them?

Every night I said that prayer, and one night I added something. I didn't plan it out or anything, it just popped out.

"Please God, make me a professional ball player."

After I said that prayer, I just sat back in awe.

What had I just done?

I'd gone and asked this higher being for a favor. Asking God to look out for loved ones seemed like asking for a good thing because other people benefit.

But this one, well, this one was all for me.

Was it wrong?

I knew I had to be something when I grew up.

And given the choice, I would eat, breathe, sleep, and bathe in sports rather than almost anything else in the world. I didn't feel like the doctor/lawyer route was my thing.

Why not be a professional ball player?

It certainly made me happy.

At the age of nine, I had a lifetime goal.

I didn't have many friends who could say the same thing.

⁖⁖⁖

Unfortunately, my attitude at school after a summer of All Stars didn't improve. After all, I'd spoken to the Man in Charge, the Guy Upstairs. I was going to be a pro ball player one day, so what did I need with school anymore?

Mom got wise to me ignoring the importance of school. She knew that all she had to do was threaten my ability to play baseball and I fell into line pretty quickly.

Things weren't going so well for Ron and my mom financially. My fourth grade year marked the first time I found myself on Reduced Lunch. Where all the other kids were paying a buck twenty-five, I was paying thirty-five cents. Every time I went through the line, I tried to hide the fact that all I was giving the lunch lady was a quarter and a dime. All the other kids were handing over a dollar bill and a quarter. It was hard to hide the difference.

"Hey Thomas! How come you don't have to pony up an extra buck like the rest of us?"

I'd seethed but I tried to just ignore the taunts.

"His mom's just a maid. They don't have enough money to pay for a full lunch."

"My mom's not a maid!" My mom had worked for years cleaning houses for other people. There were even times when I helped her. What I didn't like was the idea of her being a maid, like she was somebody's servant.

"She cleans other people's toilets. She's a maid!" This led to a scuffle right there in the lunch line. I wasn't going to stand there and let anyone insult my mom.

CHAPTER 11

Field Trip, What Can Go Wrong?

The only real difference in fourth grade for me academically was the fact that I got Mrs. Rogers as a teacher. Mrs Rogers had the reputation of being the hardest teacher at my elementary school. My first day in her classroom I was actually terrified.

But before too long I figured something out.

Mrs. Rogers didn't care about my past reputation. She didn't care about anyone's past reputation. What she cared about was how we showed up in her class this year.

In my mind, that made Mrs. Rogers one of the best teachers I ever had in my life.

She was stern and focused, and she had exactly the same expectations for every single student in her classroom.

I also knew that she would punish every kid exactly the same way for breaking one of her rules.

As a result, I stopped breaking her rules.

For the first time in my school life a teacher treated me fairly.

I could respect a teacher like that.

There was absolutely no favoritism on her part, no dwindling of her expectations. She was exactly the same for every single student in her classroom. She was extremely hard, but she was also extremely forgiving.

Each time I messed up in her classroom, I went in the next day expecting the eye roll, the look that said, "Oh Thomas, here we go again."

Not Mrs. Rogers.

She greeted me formally and politely, just as she did with every student. Every single day was a new day in her classroom and if I wanted to improve, I could.

It's probably because of Mrs. Rogers that I was well behaved enough to actually be able to go on the annual fourth grade trip to Camp Coloma. I'd heard about the trip last year, when I was in third grade. All the fourth graders who were able to raise enough money got to spend a week away from school at camp where they panned for gold, rode horses, and generally had a good time.

I wanted to go on the Camp Coloma trip. But I knew that we probably couldn't afford it, so while I wanted to go, I didn't say anything to my mom about it. Then one day she asked me why I hadn't told her about it.

At first I pretended I didn't want to go until she said, "Thomas, sell as much candy as you can and we will pay for the rest."

That was all I needed "Are you sure, Mom?"

"Of course! I want you to go and have a good time. You deserve a chance to get away and experience this with the rest of your classmates."

I brought home all the paperwork for her to sign.

The day of our departure, I was in line for the bus, holding my backpack and sleeping bag feeling like all the other students.

Before she dropped me off Mom said, "You behave up there. Remember, you only get three chances before they send you home."

"Yes, Mom." Who was she kidding? It was like I was a new kid this year. With Mrs. Rogers as my teacher, my grades were better. I wasn't acting out in class. I never missed a day of school because I enjoyed it so much.

We arrived at Camp Coloma, dropping our gear at the bunkhouse tent and then we got a taste of what life was like during the Gold Rush of 1849. We got a chance to build a shelter, I watched the kids who wanted to wash laundry. For me it was too much like what my mother did for a living. I wasn't interested. But learning how to make cornbread was fun. What I could hardly wait for, however, were the gold panning lessons.

We had been told there was gold in that sand and I was going to find it.

Think about it.

That could be the end of all our problems. I could just see myself coming home with enough gold to tell Mom she didn't have to work ever again.

Ever.

I panned for gold with the same kind of intensity and dedication that I applied to my sporting events. Even the teacher chaperones and counselors laughed at me to lighten up, but this was serious business to me. "Thomas," they said, "most of the people in 1849 didn't strike it rich!"

I didn't care. Some of them did, and I was determined to be another someone who struck it rich by panning for gold. By the end of the first day I was pleasantly tired. We'd had tacos for dinner and a campfire where we heard stories about the California Argonauts and how to identify real gold. I hadn't found gold today, but tomorrow was another day.

We had a hoe-down then headed to our bunkhouse to get ready for bed. There was plenty of roughhousing and I loved every minute of it.

"OK guys. 9:30. Lights out."

Yeah sure, in a little while.

I continued to roughhouse and crack jokes. The boys in my bunk were like my brothers. We told jokes, burped, farted, and laughed our heads off.

"Thomas, that means you."

I don't know if I didn't hear the chaperone, or if he just had it in for me, but the next words I heard were, "OK, Thomas. That's one strike against you. You get two more and you're going to be sent home."

My heart skipped a little beat, but there was no way they were going to send me home from this camp. Strangely enough, no one else got a mark against them. I was having far too much fun to worry about how unfair it was. My dreams that night were filled with finding riches beyond my wildest imaginings.

The next morning we were up with sun and packing our backpacks for a hike before more gold panning. Breakfast was French toast, sausage, oatmeal, and cold cereal. No one went hungry at Camp Coloma. During the day we hiked, heard more about the settlers of the area, and again, I was convinced that I would strike it rich the very next time I got to go gold panning. They told us stories about people who found gold the size of houses back in the day, convincing me that I would be the one to find a nugget that size.

My next warning came during free time when we were playing basketball. Still my old competitive self, I got beat out of a basket and because I was embarrassed I played too rough the next time I got the ball. I was called over by another teacher chaperone who made me sit out and it suddenly hit me that I had two strikes against me.

I didn't want to be sent home from camp, so for the rest of the night I was perfect. I didn't have nearly as much fun as I had the night before, but I didn't want to get sent home before camp ended.

I knew I had only one more chance to pan for gold before we left. When breakfast came, I rushed to be one of the first in line. I wanted to be the first in line to pan for gold.

"Thomas!"

Oh no.

"Come here."

No! No! No!

"That's your last check. You're going home."

All I'd done was reach around a kid who couldn't make up his mind between Captain Crunch and Fruit Loops. I just wanted a box of cereal so I could go gold panning.

In shame I was marched to the office where they called my mom. I listened to the phone conversation hot with humiliation and unshed tears.

It wasn't my fault.

"Thomas, go pack your backpack and your sleeping bag and bring it back here. Your mother can't come get you, so Mrs. Collins is driving up. She'll be here in a little over an hour."

For the next hour and a half I slumped in the chair, a pile of misery. It just didn't seem fair. At school they gave me plenty of warnings before I got in trouble. Here they said three times, and it wasn't even three real things I had done wrong.

It didn't help that the teacher-chaperones already knew about me. I'd even heard them talking that morning when I got called over, "Who's in trouble? Oh, Thomas. Yes, I could have put money on the fact that he'd get sent home. I'm just surprised he made it this long. Too bad."

During the mostly silent and miserable ride home I wondered what I could have done differently. Mrs. Collins radiated fury all the way back home, while all I wanted to do was go back and hang out with my friends.

The instant I got home I called Mom as I'd been instructed. She sounded cold and hostile on the phone. "I'm very disappointed in you Thomas. You're grounded. Don't even think about going outside until I get home. In the meantime, start cleaning the house. Start with the bathroom, then the kitchen . . ." Her voice droned on and on.

I knew the drill. I had to clean the house. I had to clean my room. I had to write that I will not disobey about a thousand times.

She kept listing things.

I knew what she was doing. She wanted to give me enough things to do to keep me busy until she could get home and deal with me personally.

My mother instilled a very healthy fear in me and I knew that getting sent home from the expensive school trip for misbehaving was deserving of some of the most severe punishment she could dish out. It was a little hard to sit down to dinner that night and when I went to bed, I almost forgot to ask God to help me be a pro ball player, but just as I was falling asleep, I remembered and made sure I tacked that on to the end of my prayers. I hadn't found gold, so I still needed a plan.

The next day at school was one of the most humiliating of my entire life. Everyone knew I had been sent home from Camp Coloma.

No one had ever been sent home before.

Thank God for Mrs. Rogers.

She welcomed me the next morning just as she always did and the school day began. It was a small class and a very quiet day because the only kids in fourth grade were the ones who hadn't been able to earn enough money to pay for their trip.

Then there was me.

My mother had sacrificed to pay my way, and I'd blown it. If ever I was on a path to self-destruction, this was it. There was a part of me that wondered if it was even worth trying to be good. No matter how good I tried to be, I still managed to mess it up.

Because no one else was around, Mrs. Rogers took some time to help me understand what had happened to me. One on one, I got the chance to tell her the whole story.

"Mrs. Rogers, I didn't do this the way everyone says I did. Here's what happened." And I told her my side of the story from beginning to end.

When I was done she said, "Thomas, I believe you. But there is a bigger problem than you see. You gained two checks that you didn't need to get. So you were already at risk because of that. But let's take away those two strikes. If you hadn't gotten those two other strikes when you got that last strike against you, you would still be at camp."

She pointed out that I had pushed the envelope unnecessarily. My reputation already made people wary of me, and by acting out, they were more than ready to just believe that I was a bad kid.

⚬⊛⊛⚬

The only thing I could do was continue to focus on my school studies and really practice baseball. Ron never said anything about the Camp Coloma incident. He and Mrs. Rogers were the only two people in my life who weren't judging me.

Having such an authentic relationship with a man was infinitely important to me. Ron taught me everything he knew about baseball, but more importantly he taught me about life. He encouraged me to be the best baseball player that I could be. He reminded me that who I was as a person meant more.

He said, "You can be a great ballplayer, and be a jerk at the same time. That doesn't make you a great man."

⚬⊛⊛⚬

Near the end of school there was an argument between two kids in my fourth grade class and they decided they were going to have a fight after school.

I wasn't involved. I wasn't one of the kids fighting.

I didn't need to fight anymore.

I had a dream. I had a vision. And it was baseball.

But I made a big mistake.

I offered to be their fight announcer like Michael Buffer. Ron and I would watch boxing matches, like the Holyfield and Mike Tyson fights on pay-per-view. Those fight nights turned into parties where friends and family would gather around our tiny living room to watch the fights. Michael Buffer had one job and that was to generate as much excitement as possible when he announced the last fight of the night, the one everyone was waiting for.

"Let's get ready to R-R-R-R-U-U-U-U-U-UMLLLLLLLLEE!!!!!!!!"

How many people make thousands of dollars for nine seconds of a trademark announcement? I wanted to be Michael Buffer for this fight on the playground.

And because I needed to be at the center of everything, I didn't bother to keep my voice down. I shouted loud enough for Tyson and Holyfield themselves to have heard me.

When the teachers came around, there I was in the middle of the fight. They heard my voice as the source of the commotion and they sent all three of us to the principal's office.

I stood outside and waited thinking, "I'm an innocent bystander. I didn't do anything wrong. I was just the announcer." I was sure once they asked me what happened and heard my side of the story they would realize their mistake. I ran through the events in my head just so that I could present a very fair view of what actually happened.

When I was finally called into the principal's office she said, "Thomas, I understand that you instigated this fight."

What? Was she kidding?

"No! I didn't start anything. I wasn't even fighting. I was just the announcer!"

No one would listen to me.

Not one person heard my true innocence in that case. Sure, there had been plenty of times I'd done something that deserved punishment, but this wasn't one of them!

"Really! I was the announcer. I was saying, 'In THIS corner is Mike Ryan, and in THIS corner is Marcus Bright.' Ms. Bush, you have to believe me."

"Thomas, the only thing I believe is that you're a trouble-maker and whenever there is trouble at my school, I know that you are going to be right in the middle of it."

There was no fairness. No justice.

My mother was called. She was angry and embarrassed yet again.

I was furious.

This time, my punishment was absolute injustice.

I got suspended. Again.

I had to clean the house. Again.

I had to write sentences. Again.

Then, the worst thing that could happen to a nine-year-old boy occurred when Mom came into my room.

"Call Coach. You're done playing baseball for the season."

I begged.

I pleaded.

I did everything possible to get Mom to change her mind, but once her mind was made up, there was no changing it.

Finally I called Coach. "Coach, I'm going to miss the last games of the season."

He was quiet at first, then said, "You know that if you don't play out the season, you won't be eligible for All Stars."

"Yeah, I know. Could you talk to my mom? Maybe you could convince her to change her mind."

Even Coach was unable to get Mom to change her mind.

CHAPTER 12

Mom Showing Me The Way

My suspension from school and not being able to play All Stars cast a huge shadow on what had been the best school year of my life. It seems weird when I say it, but having Mrs. Rogers as my teacher in fourth grade helped me to believe that there were some teachers who don't give up on kids just because they come into your classroom with a reputation the way I did.

Mrs. Rogers was like an umpire of a game who carefully evaluated every single questionable play and always came up with the right call. No one ever argued with her because she was fair.

No one questioned her integrity.

The end of fourth grade marked the end of my school improvement. I didn't care anymore.

Having baseball taken away from me took away my very reason for living. Nothing I said or did got Mom to change her mind.

Once I lost it, I realized that having public acknowledgment was really important to me. When there were fans in the seats watching me play ball, and if I could hit the ball further than I had ever hit it before, then I would go down as being remembered, at least by those people, that day.

Now my chance of that kind of recognition was gone because I wasn't going to be in the line-up.

Part of me wanted to act out as a result. If they all thought I was in the fight, maybe next time I should just fight. I got in so much trouble for something I didn't do.

At first I got calls from my teammate friends, "Thomas, we didn't see you at the baseball game. Where were you?"

My mom sure knew what she was doing.

That kind of public humiliation at having to explain why I couldn't play anymore was a better punishment than anything she had ever thought up before. I spent the better part of the summer alternately sulking and playing games of ball at the park, the kind without rules and without coaching. It kept me active, but it wasn't feeding my need to be noticed by people who would be impressed with my athletic abilities.

⚬⚭ ⚮⚬

Fifth grade and I didn't get along. My new teacher believed all the bad stories about me before I ever arrived in her classroom.

I spent a lot of time in the hallway, with the principal, or faking illness in the nurse's office.

⚬⚭ ⚮⚬

One day, Mom came home and announced, "I'm done. I don't want to keep cleaning houses for people. I want to do something better for myself."

Ron was fully supportive of her decision, and Mom enrolled in a local tech college where she started working on a Medical Assistant degree. Mom's decision to do something to better her life reminded me of my nightly request, that God make me a professional athlete.

Even though I didn't want to, I began to try harder in school. As a result Mom and I spent evenings doing homework together.

Seeing my mom work so hard to study and better herself made me work harder than I'd ever done before. I was still getting so-so grades, but with her showing me by example, I began to get my homework done. Some nights she had so much homework herself that she didn't have time to cook dinner. I even had to start doing the dishes because she was still studying.

As I washed and dried the dishes, I watched her in admiration. She didn't complain about how much homework she had. She just sat down and did it. I tried to copy her example, but without a teacher like Mrs. Rogers, I had little reason to work any harder. I did manage to get through most of the year without another Camp Coloma type of disaster.

In spring when baseball season came around, Mom felt I'd improved enough in the classroom that she let me play baseball again and to make up for lost time I played harder, practiced longer than ever before.

School ended and I made All Stars.

The summer before sixth grade was all baseball again. On the field I felt alive with fans in the seats, cheering when I hit a home run. Nothing nourished me quite like that sound. Then as quickly as it arrived, baseball season was over, summer ended and sixth grade loomed.

Going into sixth grade meant one thing for me.

I was finally going to be the big man on campus at my school. I'd been teased and tormented plenty of times when I was in one of the lower grades, but being a sixth grader meant I owned the school. I'd watched the hierarchy at the school from the time I was in kindergarten, and being in sixth grade meant I finally called the shots.

For the first time in my life, Mom bought me a popular pair of sneakers. Usually we shopped for the least expensive shoes because that was all we could afford, but for sixth grade Mom got me two pairs of sneakers. One pair I wore with pride and never wore them out to recess because I didn't want to get them all beat up. For recess I changed into my crummier shoes. And kids noticed that I finally wore cool shoes. Finally I felt valid, I fit in.

As a sixth grader, I intended to leave a legacy at my school. For Alamo Elementary School, I felt like I was the ultimate Hall of Fame kid because of my athletic ability on the playground.

In my mind, being a twelve-year-old sixth grader meant I didn't have to listen to anybody.

This was my last year at Alamo. On the playground, at every sporting event, every recess, every lunch period, every time I had a chance to break free from the classroom would be mine. I knew that all the younger kids would be watching me because that's what I had done when I was a younger kid. My entire time at Alamo Elementary I could hardly wait until I was in sixth grade, so I could rule the school. No one would dominate me on the basketball court. No one was going to step in front of me in the tether-ball line.

The week before school started my friends and I rode our bikes over to the school to see who we would have as a teacher. It was a fun two-mile bike ride, one I'd taken every school day for the past three years on my way to and from Alamo Elementary. We wanted to see who our new teachers were for the year so we knew ahead of time if we had to actually turn in all our homework or not. Word got around fast about teachers.

I checked the first list, hoping to be in one teacher's classroom because I knew she was pretty much a pushover.

Nope. Not there.

And not the next.

There was my name.

I had Mr. Truman.

Mr. Truman?

I had seen him around school because he was a pretty big guy, so he was hard not to miss. I wasn't too worried, but once I got home I called asking my friends who were going into seventh grade what they thought of Mr. Truman.

That's when I should have started getting worried. Instead, I got glowing reports about him.

"Thomas, you'll love him! He's so easy to get along with."

"He lets you do anything you want."

What good news for me. It was beginning to look like I was going to just be able to skate through sixth grade without any problems. What a great feeling of domination. After an unremarkable fifth grade, I was looking forward to sixth grade now.

My past experience had been to give my teachers the first two weeks of the year to get comfortable with me before I would just go back to my normal behavior, the behavior that got me attention but also got me into trouble. Mr. Truman sounded like an easy-going guy, so my expectations were for a smooth-sailing year.

I sauntered into his classroom and gave him a casual two-fingered wave. Did he see me or not? Mr. Truman seemed to be watching all the students file into his room, but his face was a mask toward me.

That made me uneasy. With good reason.

By the second week of class there was no doubt about it, Mr. Truman had it in for me. Reading aloud had never been one of my favorite activities and he picked up on that immediately. Popcorn reading became my most hated activity in school. We all read from the same book at our seats and Mr. Truman called on the first student to read. Then, right in the middle of that student reading he would say, "Popcorn, Suzie." Suzie would read for a little bit, then he would say, "Popcorn, Mike." And on and on. Mr. Truman used this method of reading aloud to keep all of us on track and reading without losing focus.

I hated reading out loud.

I never read. My insecurity about how to say certain words made me feel inferior. Mr. Truman liked to pick on me first, so I had to start reading. Once he knew I hated reading out loud, he either called on me to read, or he threatened to have me read, probably just to keep me quiet.

Pretty soon, when the reading period started, I began to ask to be excused from the classroom to go to the bathroom.

After two times, Mr. Truman got wise to me. "Thomas, you have already been to the bathroom. No, you can just stay here in class. No one else wants to be here today either, so you just plant yourself in your seat and pay attention."

He didn't like that I was trying to find ways to keep him from watching me all the time, and later it got even worse. It went from watching me just waiting for me to mess up, to actively making fun of me.

Here I was, a sixth grade student, feeling bullied by my teacher.

Who did he think he was? He knew nothing about me or my circumstances and what I have had to deal with in life so far. All he knew was what he'd seen of me in the younger grades and what he'd heard from other teachers. It just made me test him more.

"Thomas, sit down and listen."

"Why? You talking, Mr. Truman?" A few giggles could be heard in the classroom.

Mr. Truman glared at me and pointed to my chair. That time I heeded the warning in his eyes, but I could feel myself being pushed to my limit. There was no way I was going to let that man push me around.

"You can stay in from recess today," from the slight smile on his face, I knew Mr. Truman had more fun in mind for me.

Sure enough, during recess, he mocked me. There were no witnesses because all the other kids had left the classroom and it was just the two of us.

"You seem to be having some trouble adjusting to my class this year."

"Nope." I wasn't having any trouble, he was the problem.

"Let's get one thing clear. I'm the teacher and you're going to behave in my classroom or we're in for a very long year together." Who was he kidding? It was only the beginning of October and it already felt like the school year should be ending.

One day, Mr. Truman played the dirtiest trick he could have played on me. Observant man that he was, he soon figured out that my weak spot was how defensive I was of my mother. She was the most important and precious person in my life.

For history class we knew we had a movie because everything was set up for it. Mr. Truman went over to the light switches and was about to turn the lights off before starting the movie, but then he turned and announced to the classroom, "I guess we won't be turning out the lights for the movie today. Thomas is afraid of the dark and will want to call his mommy."

The whole classroom broke out into jeering laughter. My cheeks burned, and my lips twisted into a grimace of contempt and hatred. I wanted to charge out of my seat and butt the man in the stomach with my head. I wanted to knock him down and beat his face into a pulp.

Instead, I looked at my desk and pretended I couldn't hear the residual giggling. I knew he was acting out the part of a caring teacher, but it was designed to only poke more fun at me.

From that point on, he had me.

Any time I made a smart-mouthed comment in class and my classmates would laugh, he would come back with his zingers, "Maybe you need to call your mommy for that one, Thomas."

There was pretty much an unspoken rule in elementary school; you don't make fun of someone's mom.

Mr. Truman had completely violated that sacred pact. He had no idea what Mom and I were going through.

I lost all respect for the man.

CHAPTER 13

"He'll Be a Drug Dealer or He'll Be Dead"

arent-teacher conferences had never been my favorite time of year, and that year I felt the usual tightening in my gut when I knew my mom would be face-to-face with Mr. Truman. Continuing to protect her, I never told her what Mr. Truman had been doing in the classroom, but I worried what he might say to her face.

Her new job as a medical assistant made it easier for her to schedule time for parent-teacher conferences. I waited at home, not doing much of anything, dreading the moment she came home. We had many years of parent-teacher conference debriefings under our belts. With the way things were going with Mr. Truman, I didn't expect anything different.

Yet when Mom came home, she just started making dinner without saying anything to me.

Something was up.

I helped her set the table, hoping she'd notice how helpful I was being. Normally she would hug me and say, "Thank you for helping, Thomas." That night she didn't even notice. She did everything as if she were in a cloud. Even Ron looked at me a couple of times during dinner, but all I could do was shrug my shoulders back at him.

I had no idea what was wrong.

Finally, when it was time for bed, Mom came into my bedroom and sat on my bed.

"I talked to Mr. Truman today."

I didn't say anything. My teachers rarely had anything good to say about me, so I had learned to just keep my mouth shut.

"Do you want me to tell you what your teacher told me about you today?"

Not really.

I had heard everything before and none of it made me feel better about myself. This time I could tell by looking at Mom's face there was something different. My stomach clenched. Had Mr. Truman said something derogatory to my mom?

She was going to tell me, I could see it in her face. "Mr. Truman told me that by the time you are sixteen," her eyes started filling up with tears, "you will either be a leader in a gang, a drug dealer, or you'll be dead."

Then she started to cry in earnest. All I could do was hug her.

"No Mom! That will never happen." My heart really hardened against my teacher. How dare he torment my mother that way? It was one thing to tell my mother that I was disruptive in class, or that I talked back, but to tell her that I was heading down a road of total self-destruction infuriated me.

He made my mom feel as though my life was in danger. He made her feel like a failure.

I had hoped that he would tell my mom that I was improving in my studies, that I was a hard worker, that my classmates liked me. Any kid wants approval and I was no different. I wanted mom to say, "Son, I'm proud of you."

I had hoped he would tell my mom I was doing better. But what he said was much, much worse.

No way was Mr. Truman going to be right. I didn't know how, but I knew I would do everything in my power to prevent him from being right.

He will not win.

I said this over and over and over to myself until I finally fell asleep. As soon as I woke up the next morning, I was determined that Mr. Truman knew nothing about my future.

I continued to behave as if nothing had changed in his classroom. Mr. Truman wanted my mom to get me to change my ways, to make things easier on him in the classroom. I knew that. So I continued to act up. I was as disruptive as I ever. I enjoyed being the class clown, and my classmates laughed more than ever at my antics.

But, always, in the back of my mind, I kept in my thoughts that my teacher would one day eat his words.

You may not like me or respect me, Mr. Truman, but at the end of the day, you will remember my name.

Mr. Truman's opinion of me was completely different from the way I saw myself. I had plenty of people who thought I was a good kid and fun to be around. My teammates loved having me on their teams. I was always one of the first ones called when an impromptu game was being set up.

People liked me.

Didn't that make me a normal kid? I'd seen plenty of other kids getting into trouble, being disciplined. How did that make me any different?

As the year went on, however, I did pay a whole lot more attention to how people treated me and how they treated other kids. I began to see that while I was called to join a sporting event, I wasn't invited so much to things like birthday parties. Every now and again, when she was especially exasperated with me Mom would say, "Thomas, you're just like your father."

Inside my head I wanted to shout, "I am not just like him! I never want to be like him!" But was it possible she was right? Had some of those traits that I didn't admire in my dad rubbed off on me?

I realized in general, no one really liked me. They enjoyed my athletic abilities, but as a person, they didn't like me.

We've all heard and laughed at people going through a mid-life crisis. Now it wasn't funny anymore. Here I was in sixth grade and going through such a crisis. My teacher figured I was a hoodlum and my mother was afraid I'd be killed in a gang fight. I don't even know where that came from. I might throw gang signs, but every guy in my school did that.

It was cool. But it didn't mean anything.

Did it?

Part of me feared that Mr. Truman might be right about my future. I had to stuff that fear deep down inside, because if I thought about it too much, I began to think that it didn't matter what I did to better myself.

What would happen if I just didn't care? What if I stopped trying, stopped fighting to be better? I could just be lazy and complacent.

Thoroughly confused, I pulled into myself.

I'm not sure that I really noticed it at first, but I found myself looking to spend more time with Ron where we would go play catch or to the batting cages. I'd wait until no one was around, and then I would shoot basketball hoops by myself. And, much to my mom's great pleasure, I really applied myself to doing chores. It was something I could do by myself, and I knew how to do them well.

Every time Mom came home to a clean kitchen or sparkling bathroom, she would say, "Oh, Thomas! What a great job you did!" That's what I was looking for. Approval and appreciation.

By focusing on doing things alone, I developed a very strong drive to motivate myself. I polished the sink until it gleamed, and no one had to stand over my shoulder and tell me I missed a spot. At the batting cage, I would swing as hard as I could.

Again.

Again and again.

No one had to encourage me to keep it up. I kept it up all by myself.

If kids didn't want to spend time with me, well it was just their loss. "Someday," I whispered to myself, "they'll pay attention and wish they were still my friend. I'll show all of them how wrong they are."

After a while, Mom started nagging me to call friends. "Thomas, you shouldn't spend so much time by yourself. Go out and play with some of your friends." Her pestering irritated me, as I was playing a video game and had just gotten to the top level. Not having to share with someone else allowed me to become really, really good at what I was doing.

"I will in a minute."

"You used to play with all the kids in the neighborhood. What happened?"

"Nothing happened." Right, nothing happened. Mr. Truman happened, that's what happened, but I couldn't bring that unhappy memory up to my mom. What had happened, however, was that sometimes I saw a little of what Mr. Truman warned Mom about. I found myself admitting that my thoughts and beliefs in myself weren't adding up to the person I wanted to be.

No way was I going to admit that Mr. Truman was right.

He was going to eat his words one day. I just had to figure out how to make that happen. Ever since that night there was a fire that grew inside me and I kept it close to my heart. No way was my mother going to sacrifice her life to give the best she possibly could and have me end up getting shot or being the leader of a gang somewhere.

I knew in my heart I was destined for better things than that. I maintained a certain uneasy equilibrium for the remainder of my sixth grade year with Mr. Truman. My final report card was one C, one A, and the rest were B's. My behavior was considered unsatisfactory. I got a C-minus in citizenship and I didn't demonstrate responsibility. As far as Mr. Truman was concerned, I passed his class but I was still a drain on society.

His words haunted me for a very long time. I would watch on the news how the cops chased down gang members who were usually carrying a gun or a knife. Did that mean I had to carry a gun or a knife? It's not something I'd admit to any of my classmates, but the idea of guns scared me. But if Mr. Truman was right, I'd have to be one up on everyone, and that meant I had to carry a gun. And the drugs . . . I didn't want to take drugs.

But what if Mr. Truman were right?

I felt like I was drowning, and I couldn't ask anyone for help because that might mean they would drown right along with me. Besides, I was a man, and as a man, if you fall down, you get up, dust yourself off and try it again.

What was going on inside my head was very different.

My mom had only one kid, and every morning I could see that small flicker of fear in her eyes that maybe Mr. Truman was right. Her fear was contagious. By the time sixth grade ended, I wondered if I had what it took to become the person I dreamed about.

One night after a baseball game, Mom and I were driving home. I looked out the window I saw all the lights of the hamburger places flickering below us, giving it the name Hamburger Hill.

"There's nothing for me here," I whispered.

"What did you say, Thomas?" Mom asked.

"Nothing."

There really was nothing I could say out loud to Mom that wouldn't further alarm her or make her more afraid for me. But I knew that I had to get myself out of Vacaville. I had to get some kind of scholarship and get myself out by either going to college or playing on a pro ball team.

My nightly prayers continued, and I still asked God every night to please let me be a pro ball player.

Now, my prayers intensified.

"Please God, let me be a pro-ball player. I do NOT want to be in a gang, and I do NOT want to be killed."

CHAPTER 14

School Bully

With Mr. Truman and sixth grade behind me, the summer stretched out in front of me like a long, grand vacation.

No schoolwork, just play.

With my growing prowess in playing baseball and being invited to play on more and more select baseball teams, it started to sink in that baseball might actually be my ticket out of Vacaville. Being one of a select few chosen to play on the higher level traveling baseball team thrilled and excited me because the team was made up of kids from all over Northern California, from Sacramento to the Bay Area.

My summer was going just great until one morning the phone rang.

"Hello?"

"Is this Thomas?" It was a voice I didn't recognize.

"Yeah."

"Hey, I'm Tiny." While I didn't recognize his voice, the name was crystal clear. Tiny was a thug, a member of a local gang family. "I hear in my neighborhood you think you are a tough S.O.B."

My blood chilled at this.

Crap!

I knew Tiny by reputation. No one messed around with his gang because you mess with one, you mess with all of them.

"What do you want?" I asked.

"When we get to Jepson, we'll find out exactly how tough you think you are. We'll see if you walk around throwing up gang signs. We'll find out."

Tiny hung up the phone.

Immediately my heart sunk into my shoes. He was right, I'd been throwing up gang signs because I thought it was cool. That's how everyone in the neighborhood played around. We copied the movements of the guys on rap videos. It didn't mean I was in a gang.

While I didn't personally know Tiny, I knew enough about him to feel deep, ice-cold fear. He was one year older than I was, and I'd heard stories about him as a sixth grader going to the middle school and beating up on the seventh and eighth graders. His family was notorious for rounding up their crew when they wanted to get back at someone.

I was tough.

I'd been called a bully at school. My size gave me a huge advantage on the playground. To have someone call me up and threaten me had never happened before.

And for the first time in my life I felt fear.

I was afraid of what this guy said he was going to do to me. I didn't want to mess with him.

He called my home, so he obviously knew where I lived.

He knew my name.

And then I thought about the one thing in my life I needed to protect even more carefully than my sports ability.

Mom.

What if Tiny and his family showed up at my house to come after me or if I wasn't home and they hurt my mom instead? Tiny's reputation around town was that he was a seriously tough guy.

Mr. Truman's words echoed around in my head. "He's either going to be in a gang, or he's going to be dead."

The thing was, I didn't want to be either. In a gang, or dead.

Tiny's call scared me. I feared for my life. But more importantly, I needed to protect my mom from this situation.

A week or two went by with no further word from Tiny.

School started in a week, and my fear continued to grow to the point I couldn't eat, couldn't sleep.

"Thomas, you feeling OK?" Mom asked me one morning when I refused breakfast yet again.

"Yeah." I'd struggled to figure a way out of the threat Tiny had made. Then I had a brilliant idea. "What if we were to move to a different house, different school before school starts?"

Sure. That would solve my problem and I wouldn't have to tell Mom that we'd been threatened by gang members.

I wanted to move.

I wanted to change schools.

I wanted to cut and run.

Mom laughed. "Thomas, we can't move right now. Why would you want to move? You're already going to a new school. You should be excited."

I had been excited about going to Jepson.

Until that phone call.

Now I was terrified.

I finally told Mom about the call and she notified the principal, saying that if anything happened to me she was going to hold the school responsible.

What good that did, I don't know.

It didn't make me feel any better.

Mom had read a book by Maya Angelou about someone threatening her family. As a result, Maya Angelou's mother carried a little pistol to protect herself and her child. Because she and Ron had recently broken up, Mom considered getting a gun to protect us.

What had I done? The only way to solve this problem was to get a gun?

While Mom considered the gun, she instead chose to stick up for me by notifying the principal.

I sure hoped she was right.

⁂

Despite all my school experiences, usually I looked forward to the first day of school, much like most kids. But instead of worrying about what clothes I was going to wear to make a good impression on my teachers, I spent my time just trying to figure out what I was going to do when I saw Tiny.

Back in sixth grade, I considered myself to be the toughest kid in my school. Now I was terrified of a kid I hadn't even met yet, but who was notorious for beating people up.

Before this, I had never been threatened off of the ball field. On the ball field, there were a lot of things you could do to other players, but it had to fall within the rules of the game.

Here, at school, there were no rules when it came to gang activity. That was what I found terrifying.

I couldn't exactly run if I saw the guy coming down the hall between classes.

What would I do?

Fight him?

If I fought him, what happened if I won? That only opened up another can of worms because then his family and friends would come after me.

The first day of school arrived and again Mom was stunned that I couldn't eat breakfast. Before being threatened by Tiny I always had a huge appetite for breakfast.

"You'll be starved by lunchtime. You're just a little nervous about your first day at a new school."

I let her think that. I didn't want to remind Mom about the gang threat at school.

I crept into school and tried to make myself as invisible as possible. Unlike elementary school, middle school didn't have home room classrooms. We moved from class to class during passing period, sometimes running to the lockers to change out books, before rushing back in time to be in the room when class started.

Added to that chaos was the ever-present fear that I'd run into Tiny and my life would be over. In middle school I learned a lot more about gangs and gang activity than I'd ever known before.

Almost daily there were stories throughout the nation of stabbings, shootings, and how gangs rolled in packs terrorizing neighborhoods.

And there I was, running from a gang member all because he'd seen me acting like a big shot and throwing gang signs. I didn't even know what they meant.

Everyone did it.

But Tiny's phone call taught me that if you throw the signs, then you better be prepared to deal with the consequences of throwing them. Only I wasn't a gang member and I didn't have a territory.

But try telling that to a gang member.

To them, it's all a contest to be the toughest guy around and I did have that reputation at Alamo Elementary.

Maybe Mr. Truman was right, that I would get stabbed or shot in seventh grade.

Every day I woke up with my stomach clenched in fear. I'd never been so consistently afraid before in my life.

For the first month of school, as soon as the final bell rang, I ran home as fast as I could. I still hadn't seen Tiny and I didn't know who he hung with. Not knowing who your enemy is makes it hard to make friends so I only spent time with the kids I already knew from my previous school.

My biggest fear was to have a confrontation with Tiny and his friends on the school grounds. Once that happened, everyone would crowd around. Kids in middle school can't resist a fight, and I had no problem with fighting as long as I knew I had a chance of winning. A gang fight usually involved more than fists.

Self-doubt was a new emotion for me and I wasn't sure I liked it. It had a lot more control over me than I ever thought it could. I couldn't focus on school.

Tiny's threat hung over me and pretty much ruined my entire first semester at Jepson.

One day in class, I needed to be excused to go to the restroom. And it wasn't me making up an excuse to get out of class. That year classrooms were my refuge. But nature called and I had no choice but to respond.

I walked out of the classroom and turned down Hallway A, then turned right again down Hallway B which was nothing but rows of lockers on either side of the hallway.

And one student walking my way.

Tiny.

My heart stopped.

I couldn't breathe.

Here it was.

Our first face-to-face confrontation. There was no way I could just turn around and run back into the classroom.

I decided to brave it out and just kept walking, my head down, not making eye contact with Tiny.

I'd just passed him when he turned around and said, "Thomas?"

"Yeah?" I just stopped and looked at his shoulder. No way I was looking him in the eye. I didn't want to challenge him in any way in the hallway with no witnesses.

He put out his hand. Just an ordinary hand shake. "Tiny."

I took his hand, thinking he was going to sucker punch me. "Yeah."

"We're cool, man. Sorry about the phone call last summer. I thought you were trying to come in and run Jepson. We're cool."

I later learned he had asked around about me. "Is Thomas a gang-banger?" People told him, "No, the complete opposite. He's no threat."

And just like that the weight of the world fell off my shoulders.

In a split second all the terror, the pain, the self-imposed imprisonment, the concern for my mother's safety melted away like ice on a hot skillet.

As I walked back to my classroom after using the restroom I marveled at how I had allowed fear to rule my life for so long.

I let my fear of this moment to keep me from eating, from going outside to play, from meeting new people. All because I didn't want to get beat up.

I vowed then to never allow fear to rule my life again.

Sure, things might turn out as bad as you think, but sometimes it turns out to be nothing. Like Tiny. I'd wasted so many days worrying about it.

I lost half a year of my life for nothing.

CHAPTER 15

Who Am I?

Once my close call with Tiny and his gang family ended, I was finally able to focus on being a middle school kid. I'd missed half the year being afraid of what might happen, and I hadn't spent a lot of time deciding who I wanted to hang out with.

Everyone in middle school is looking for their identity, and you have quite a lot of choices. For me, I felt I wasn't black enough for some kids, and wasn't white enough for others. I certainly wasn't a nerd. Goths were just too out there for me, and while I was very athletic, I hadn't found any groups of sports-related friends yet.

One day a couple kids approached me, some in my grade, a couple in eighth grade. "We're going to ditch third period. Meet us at the bridge behind the school."

Wow. It felt good to be wanted. I knew ditching school wasn't a great idea, but it was for just one period, so I decided to enjoy myself after my self-imposed imprisonment the first semester. They said they'd share a joint with me.

I liked the idea of being a part of a group. I'd been so isolated for months that to be included felt wonderful. I wanted to be part of something.

When time came to meet, I threw all my books and backpack in my locker and ran as fast as I could so that I wouldn't be late.

Once the bell rang, you had eight minutes to get from one class to the next. I made my escape in the chaos of class change and just prayed that no one saw me.

As I got closer to the bridge I wondered if I was going to get in trouble once I went back to school. Then I began to wonder if the guys who had invited me would even be there.

It was possible that they pranked me. I slowed my pace as I got closer to the bridge. Not wanting to appear too eager and out of breath, I strolled the rest of the way to the bridge over a creek. The surrounding woods hid us from view of the school.

As I approached, one kid pulled what looked like a misshapen cigarette out of his backpack. Another kid said, "Fire it up."

He lit it with the lighter from his pocket and it sparked the joint. One by one, each kid put it to their mouth and inhaled the smoke, eyes closed, heads nodding. When it finally reached me, I realized what a knucklehead I was. They were doing drugs.

I wanted to be part of something. I wanted to hang out. I didn't want to do drugs.

But I was there and didn't want to look like a chump. So, I took the joint, put it to my mouth and let some of the smoke enter my mouth. I refused to inhale it. I just held my breath, holding the smoke in my mouth, and then blew it out after a few seconds to make it look like I was participating just like the other kids.

There wasn't really much talking. They weren't doing anything but watching the joint get smaller and smaller as it kept going around the group. My relief that it was gone before it got around to me a second time told me that I really didn't want to be part of this group. Once the joint was gone, some kids went home, some went to 7/11.

I went back to school. Alone again.

I heard the bell, which meant I had exactly eight minutes to get my books and into my next class without getting caught.

I flew back to the school, raced to my locker, grabbed my history book and made it to fourth period history just in time.

When I took my seat I imagined my mom sitting next to me, just looking at me. I could see the disappointment in her eyes. I'd let her down by making a bad choice. I could even hear her voice saying, "Didn't we just have this conversation? You know how much I'm struggling to keep things together for us. And now you go and do this? Do you know how disappointed I am in you?"

I felt guilty about skipping class for a long time.

෩෧ ๑෨

I met Fabian during baseball season. Fabian was a phenomenal athlete, a pitcher, a ladies' man, and a really good looking kid. He was the picture perfect All-American kid, slicked back hair, tall, handsome, and a really excellent ballplayer.

I wanted like anything to be his friend.

One night after a game we hung around talking and I asked Mom if he could spend the night. Mom was always giving me opportunities to hang out with friends, so he was allowed to stay the night. Mom got some snacks and video games for us, made us dinner and after everything was cleaned up she went to bed.

Fabian and I watched television and played video games and I was really excited that the most popular kid at school was spending the night at my house.

At one point, Fabian got up and went and listened at my mom's bedroom door.

"What are you doing?" I asked.

"Just checking that your mom's asleep."

I knew she was asleep. She worked so hard that when she put lights out, she went to sleep quickly.

"Do you have any alcohol?"

"Huh? Alcohol?"

"Do you have any alcohol?" he repeated.

I had never seen my mom drink. I knew my dad drank. If he'd asked me at Dad's house, I would know exactly where the alcohol was.

I just shook my head at Fabian. I had no idea if Mom had any alcohol in the house.

Fabian went into the kitchen and started going through the cabinets, quietly, but each tink of glass made my heart stop. I didn't want him to be searching through our kitchen, but I didn't want him to think I was a square.

"Ha! Found some!" Fabian came through the darkness toward me, he had the top off a bottle and took a long drink straight from the bottle. "Here, take a chug."

I shook my head. I didn't want to do this, any more than I'd participated in the joint smoking on the bridge.

But I didn't want him telling everyone at school that I was a wuss or a sissy. I took the bottle, breathed deep to prepare myself and took a chug.

The first drink burned all the way down to my stomach. I almost choked. My throat was on fire. But when Fabian took another chug and handed it back to me, I took another, and another, until the bottle was about empty.

My head spun. I felt lightheaded. I couldn't stand straight, and when I walked, I bumped into the couch, and then fell onto the cushions. We smothered our laughter. I was having fun, but deep down I still knew this was something I shouldn't be doing.

Fabian went back into the kitchen where I heard the refrigerator door open and then a cabinet closing. I didn't see how he could want anything to eat after drinking all that alcohol. My stomach churned unhappily.

"What are you doing?"

"Nothing."

I either passed out or just fell asleep until the next morning.

After that sleepover, Fabian and I didn't ever talk about the incident again, and I promptly forgot about it.

A week before the Christmas holidays I was spending the night at Todd's house. Mom approved of Todd because he was a good student and I think she hoped some of his good study habits might rub off on me. I had been to Todd's home numerous times and I often managed to spend not one but two nights there.

This time, however, Todd's mom woke us up early the first morning of my sleepover. "Thomas, your mom's here to pick you up."

What? I wasn't supposed to go home until tomorrow. But I didn't argue. I collected my things and went out to the car where Mom was waiting.

"Hey, Mom. Did I forget we had to be somewhere today?" It was a Saturday and I didn't think I had anything planned.

At first mom didn't say anything, just gestured with her head to get my stuff in the car. She waved to Todd's mom as we drove away.

As she drove, without looking at me, Mom asked, "What happened to the brandy bottle?"

Brandy bottle? What brandy bottle?

Then it hit me. The brandy bottle that Fabian found and we had pretty much emptied the night he stayed over.

"The what?" I stalled for time.

"The brandy bottle, Thomas. What happened?" Her voice was hard and angry. "One of the girls who came to my Christmas party last night opened up the brandy bottle and poured herself a drink. You know what she told me? She told me that wasn't brandy in that bottle. It was old Coke. Now, do you want to tell me what happened to the brandy bottle?"

I remembered drinking the brandy, but I didn't see what Fabian had done with it afterward. Obviously, though, he had filled up the brandy bottle with coke.

"Thomas, I was so embarrassed."

I slunk down in my seat.

"I'm so disappointed in you. I can't trust you."

That really hurt.

She was right. I had violated her trust by allowing the popular athlete to talk me into sneaking and drinking my mother's brandy. But to have my own mother say she didn't trust me in her house was a bitter pill to swallow. Gaining her trust back wasn't going to happen overnight.

One more point to Mr. Truman.

CHAPTER 16

Cut From The Team

The sport to play in seventh grade was basketball. There was flag football, but I still felt like flag football was a game for sissies. To me, football meant you needed to tackle, to physically take down a person. Waving a little flag around didn't have the same impact.

So I decided to play on the basketball team.

While I was very athletic, I had only played basketball on the playground or at the park. I'd never played organized basketball.

But I wanted the admiration I saw the pro ball players got at the games, with cheering crowds right on top of you, to me the pro players were like gods.

And I wanted to be just like them.

I noticed during tryouts that I wasn't as good as some of the other players. That was a new experience for me.

All my life, I'd always excelled at any athletics I tried.

But now I was challenged to do things that didn't come easily to me. I had to dribble with my left hand, do a left-handed layup, and most importantly I had to learn how to pass.

As tryouts continued, we got closer and closer to final cuts. I was still in, but hanging on by the skin of my teeth. For the first time in my athletic career, I was not one of the best players on the team.

The day final cuts were posted, I went with my friends to see who made it and who didn't.

The list was in alphabetical order. I started at the top and scanned down to the bottom, looking for my name.

It wasn't there.

I did not make the final cut.

My friends had made it, but I didn't.

I felt like I wasn't good enough.

I hung my head in embarrassment. My athletic prowess was my claim to fame.

Being cut from the basketball team was my first defeat ever in sports.

Mom tried to make me feel better by signing me up for recreational basketball, but everyone knew that all you had to do was pay and you were on the team. I wanted to be on a team because I was good, not because I had paid for a position.

Something had to change.

I had to change just about everything in my life because the choices I'd been making were not going to get me closer to where I wanted to be.

Watching the Jepson players in their gold and black jerseys made me want to work harder so that next season I would be good enough to play on the school team.

Life became a challenge. I'm not good enough? OK, I'll just work hard enough until I'm good enough. That philosophy in my sports life carried over into my home life as well.

Mom constantly reminded me, "You're trying to gain my trust back, Remember? Each time I left to go to a friend's house where she wasn't going to be supervising me she would remind me, "Don't do anything you shouldn't." I was determined to earn her trust back. I wanted her to just know that I would make the right decisions.

So when I was invited to join the group of kids at the bridge again, I started telling white lies about having a project or a paper due. I didn't want them to make fun of me or think I was a wuss.

I didn't want to appear uncool.

But I also wanted Mom to be really proud of me. I understood how hurt she was when she was embarrassed in front of her friends.

I knew what it was like to be embarrassed in front of your friends because I knew how I felt when my friends made fun of me when they found out my mom used to clean houses.

It would take a real idiot not to see how hard Mom worked to make a life for us. Other friends had dads who ran the barbecue and mowed the lawn. Mom did all jobs at our house because she loved me, and repaying her the way I'd been repaying her the past few months just wasn't cutting it.

I actually didn't need her telling me I had to improve my behavior. Deep inside my own gut, I knew.

I started to care about how well I did in school. Mom would say, "Why can't you get good grades like Grant, or Phil, or Todd?"

Those were my inner circle friends. To have Mom point out that I wasn't as good a student as they were was like getting cut from the basketball team because I wasn't good enough.

Seventh grade taught me that I must do better than I'd been doing or Mr. Truman was going to be right.

And that was never going to happen.

⚜

Before I knew it, eighth grade had started and still I focused on sports. I'd been scouted at the end of seventh grade to play traveling baseball with a select group of thirteen-year-olds who represented Northern California called NorCal. To me this was a big deal because the scout was a Philadelphia Phillie's scout. We were talking major league baseball. I thought his attention and getting on the NorCal team would put me in the pipeline to professional baseball.

He met with my mom and me explaining that most kids who go to the Major League level don't usually get in through normal community recreational ball. The way to get seen was by participating in and doing well on the traveling teams because the level of competition was higher and we played against a lot of really good athletes from all over the country.

We practiced in the Bay area but our games were played all along the coast of California, in Arizona, Oklahoma, and Tennessee. That was the best experience of my life, hopping on planes with my baseball gear with fifteen other guys. Without traveling baseball, I wouldn't have seen all those parts of the country.

If it hadn't been for Ron, giving me the opportunity and exposure, I don't think I would have been able to have that experience. Mom and Ron helped me foot the bill for those trips, and they even came on the trips with me. Ron's love of baseball paled in comparison to his love of watching me do something that I loved.

My biggest fear at that point was watching my dreams potentially disappear. While I had been one of the very best players on my previous baseball teams, on the traveling team, I discovered my abilities were barely average.

To move on to the big leagues, I had to be the fastest runner, the strongest batter, and able to throw the ball the farthest. And as hard as I tried, there were a lot of guys who were just better than I was. In fact, it seemed that no matter what I did, I never improved enough. I was doing all the extra work, but the gap continued to grow. At the age of thirteen and fourteen, those kids were hitting baseballs as far as grown men and making plays like you might see on ESPN SportsCenter.

Up until that point, I'd always been told that I was the best in baseball.

Every team I'd ever been on.

Every game I'd ever played.

Those words came from the coaches, the parents, other players. Everyone had constantly told me that I'd be a major league ball player, and I figured that was how I was going to get out of Vacaville as a professional athlete.

And yet, I wasn't outshining the players on the traveling teams. While I loved the camaraderie, the brotherhood of traveling with my friends on the team, my confidence in my athletic abilities was severely shaken that summer.

To get better at something, you have to humble yourself enough to ask for help. I didn't have that kind of humility.

I just watched them.

I watched the way they prepared, the way they practiced, how professionally they approached their craft, the way they would touch their glove, how they put on their shoes and cleats. To me, they personified all that I loved about the game. But I knew, I just knew, I wasn't as good as they were on the diamond.

They were ahead of me and I didn't know if I could ever catch up.

But it never occurred to me to quit the team. My teammates were my brothers, and I knew when I went back to regular baseball, I'd still get the praise and worship as before.

On a regular team, I was definitely the star player. And I really liked that.

But was it enough?

ﻌﻟﻪ ﻌﻟﻪ

We all carve out who we think we are and find others in school who are interested in the same things.

"I'm a ballplayer," is what I'd say anytime anyone asked who I was. That was my identity and I hung out with other athletes during passing periods and before and after school.

We were all athletes.

To lose my identity as an athlete scared me.

I'd been figuring out how to do better, be better at school, and still I didn't want to apply myself any more than I had to. My grades improved a little, but not enough to satisfy my mom who regularly told me, "You can do better, Thomas."

She was probably right, but being an athlete meant I focused on working as hard as I could on my abilities on the field or on the court. I'd been practicing basketball so that I could finally make the team after my humiliating experience in seventh grade of not even making the team. I didn't know how to do both, athletics and scholastics.

At the time I had gotten cut from seventh grade basketball, I figured there was something wrong with the coaches and their perception. I even had the nerve to ask the coach why my friends had made the team and I had been cut. That coach was brutally honest and he listed all my flaws. He'd compare me to the other guys on the team saying things like, "Jeremy can dribble with his left hand, Mike plays good defense, and Jared knows how to make a left-handed layup. You can't do any of those things."

I thought it was just a pass-and-shoot game. After the coach brutally pointed out my deficits, I went home and practiced in my front yard on the hoop that I weighed down with water and rocks to keep it from falling over when the winds blew.

My efforts paid off. I made the basketball team in eighth grade. Seeing my name on that final roster gave me a sense of pride, accomplishment, achievement.

I had done it!

But even though I had made it onto the basketball team, I was still only the seventh or eighth man coming off the bench.

I didn't want to be the seventh or eighth man off the bench.

I wanted to be the starter.

I wanted to be the best player on the court.

My idea of being a star athlete didn't seem to be working.

Here I go again, I thought. I'm a J.A.G.

Just. A. Guy.

Just a guy playing basketball, thinking he's great, and yet in my heart I knew I wasn't.

⁂

More and more of my friends and acquaintances were experimenting with drugs and alcohol and while I wasn't making huge progress in school, I wasn't slipping behind the way they were. For them, ditching school became part of their daily routine. I couldn't ditch anymore because I was on the sports teams and my coaches worked at the school. They got the reports of who was in school and who wasn't. The rules were, if you missed school then you couldn't practice or play. I was double accountable for my attendance now. My coaches at school and my mom at home.

Eighth grade for me was figuring out how to be just good enough to get by.

I wanted my grades to be good enough that Mom wouldn't nag me to be better and I had grades good enough to play on the team.

I wanted to be a good enough athlete that people would recognize that I was a good athlete, but not give me grief for not being better.

On the basketball court, it was almost a standing joke that I couldn't hit a three-point shot. I probably shot thirty three-point shots that year, and I only made one of them. I felt that I had great form, I was planted right, yet once the ball left my hands it never went in the basket until the final game of the season when we played our archrival, Vaca Pena.

In my mind, I hit every basket I attempted. But in the paper the next day it said, "Williams: nine points."

I thought I had forty points. The newspaper reported otherwise.

Our minds do strange things. My mind told me that I was a much better basketball player than I really was. But the stats proved that I was lying to myself. I hadn't scored the forty points I thought I'd scored.

Was I really just a great athlete in my mind?

Was I a fake?

Would I ever get out of Vacaville as a professional athlete?

CHAPTER 17

Coaches Know Best

Eighth grade wrapped up with me being invited back for my second year on the traveling baseball team, NorCal.

Maybe this time, because I was a little older, a little bigger and stronger, I could be a better contender on the field. Last year I spent time on the bench. This year I knew I would be a starter.

I had to be.

This was the year the scouts would be coming around and looking at all the players. I needed to do something to get their attention.

I had to stand out. Be special.

Typically during the summer the kids in my neighborhood went camping, boating, or swimming.

I played ball. That was my summer vacation.

Another summer activity was freshman football.

Sure we'd just finished eighth grade, but Vacaville High regularly recruited the incoming freshmen to get together over the summer to lift weights, do strength and conditioning programs, learn how to play Bulldog football.

Not me.

No. My focus was baseball.

I identified myself as a baseball player and on the days I did not have baseball practice I had no intention of joining my friends for their football practice sessions.

The way I looked at it, this was my "make or break" year in baseball. I didn't have time to be sidetracked with football, no matter how many of my friends were playing.

A man named Ed Santopadre changed all that.

Ed Santopadre was a high school teacher and football coach. His boys had been active in sports, so I'd seen him around cheering his own kids on, and remembered they were exceptional athletes.

Midway through summer between eighth grade and my freshman year of high school the phone rang.

Mom answered. "Hello?" She listened for a moment, and then handed the phone to me.

"Hello?"

"Thomas! This is Coach Santopadre. I noticed you haven't been practicing football with the other incoming freshmen guys. I just wanted to make sure you knew you were welcome to join them to get ready to play freshman football come fall."

No way I was playing football.

Was he kidding?

I needed him to understand I was a baseball player. "Thank you very much for the phone call, Coach. I appreciate that you'd like me to play football this fall, but I have to say no. I'm going to be a professional baseball player."

"Well, that sounds good. But what are you going to do in the fall?"

"Coach, I'm very sure about what I want to do."

"Thomas, I've seen you play myself. You've got a lot of talent and I think you would be just as good on the football field. You can do both."

"Thank you, sir."

"The way I see it, you can play football during football season and you can play baseball during baseball season. They don't have to interfere with one another."

"No, I think I'm pretty sure I just want to play baseball." I said.

Coach wasn't taking my rejection. It was as if he wasn't even hearing me. "It won't take away any of your time. We just want you to get out there. I think it would be great, don't you?"

"Well, I'm sure it would, but I'm not a football player."

"Think about it. It will be fun. At least try it and if you don't like it you can change your mind."

His words still weren't reaching me. Baseball was my thing.

"No, Coach. I'm good, but thank you anyway." I'd never been so relieved to get off the phone.

Mom had been close by listening on my end of the conversation. She looked at me, "Are you sure you don't want to play football with your friends?"

"Mom, you know I'm a baseball player."

And I was. I was certain that would be my ticket out of Vacaville. And that was all that I thought about the matter.

Until Coach Santopadre called the next week.

And the week after.

And the week after that.

Like clockwork, Coach Santopadre called me every Wednesday afternoon right about lunchtime.

All summer long, he called me.

"Hey, Thomas! Just giving you a call back to see if you thought anything about joining the football team?"

"Yeah, Coach. I've thought about it. But I don't want to play football."

"Why don't you want to play?"

"Coach, I'm a baseball player. I'm going to the major leagues. It's what I've been dreaming about from the time I was a little boy."

The more I thought about it, the more I realized I was worried about getting hurt. I'd heard about football accidents, players getting hurt, concussions, broken bones. I couldn't afford to get injured and messing up my dream of becoming a professional baseball player.

After a while, when I would see Coach Santopadre's number show up on the phone display I would signal to my mom to say that I wasn't there.

And Mom would lie for me. "Sorry, Coach, Thomas isn't here right now. I'll have him call you when he gets home."

Which I never did.

And still he kept calling.

Finally, I answered the phone because Mom said she wasn't going to keep lying for me. And I'd finally come up with a good reason for not joining my friends on the football field. I was still playing baseball.

So I lied.

I lied to Coach Santopadre. "Sorry, Coach. I really can't come and practice with the football team because I'm on the NorCal team and we practice every day."

That wasn't true, but I didn't think he would find out. And I hoped it would stop the phone calls.

"That's fine, Thomas. Don't worry about it."

My relief was a physical release.

Then Coach went on to say, "As long as you tell me that you will be here the first day of practice in fall camp, we've got a spot for you."

Hello? Aren't you hearing me?

How many ways could I tell him I wasn't going to play football?

For now, though, the phone calls stopped and I could continue my summer by paying attention to my baseball skills and my video games.

⚬⚬⚬⚬

Toward the end of our summer baseball season, we traveled to Tennessee to play in a national tournament.

In the fifth inning I walked, then stole second base. A ground ball hit to right field and I was on the move, rounding third base. I charged toward home plate.

As I got closer, I noticed the catcher about three or four feet in front of the plate, blocking my path.

Every step I took brought me closer to a collision with the catcher. His body language challenged me to make him move. I lowered my shoulder to protect myself as I approached and ran him over.

A charge of adrenalin pumped through my body!

I'd never felt such a feeling before.

I could feel my soul screaming at me.

Finally!

All throughout my baseball career, I'd carefully avoided physical contact with the other players, looking to avoid injury.

But this new sensation inside of me surpassed any thrill I'd ever had on the baseball field before.

I got kicked out of the game for contacting the catcher and running him over. But back in the dugout, my team and my coaches all high-fived me. They approved of my effort. I had found a socially acceptable way to play out my aggressions.

What a strange feeling. Even though I had no intention of hurting the catcher, I still didn't pull away from trying to move him out of my way as I went for home plate.

The tingly sensation that pumped through my body lasted. It was the most exhilarated I'd ever felt on the field.

We finished in the Top Ten in the country that year and headed home.

Baseball season was over.

One night Mom and I were in the garage folding laundry after running my uniforms through the washing machine.

"Thomas, what are you going to do with your time from now until it's time to play baseball next spring in high school? You either have to get a job or find something else to do with your time."

She was right. I wouldn't be playing baseball for a good six months. Here it was July and baseball practice didn't start until January.

"I don't know, Mom." And that was the truth. I didn't know.

Suddenly a huge empty hole opened up before me, and I sure didn't want to get a job. I had nothing to do. For the first time in many years, I didn't have some kind of practice to go to.

That night, Mom came home from the grocery store. "Jimmy's mom was asking me if you were going to join the rest of the boys playing football now. I had to tell her I didn't know because you insist that baseball is all you play."

It was Mom's way of saying that she was worried, too, about how I was going to fill my time.

"Oh, I'll just hang out with my friends. You know, play down at the park."

"But Thomas, all your other friends are playing football, not playing at the park. What are you going to do? Who are you going to hang out with?"

"I really don't know, Mom." But I knew I needed to pray about it. She was right. If all my friends were at practice on the football field, I wouldn't have anyone to hang out with.

For years I'd been praying to God to help me become a professional athlete, and I'd pretty much determined that I was going to be a baseball player.

But that night, my conversation with God changed a little bit. "So God, what am I supposed to do?"

As soon as I woke up my prayers had been answered. At breakfast I said, "Mom, I'm playing football."

It was that quick. That sudden. I just knew it was the right decision. And I'd made it just in time because it was only two days before the start of football training camp.

Mom's surprise at my change of heart was evident. "When did this come about? What happened? Why did you suddenly change your mind?" She wanted to be sure that I understood my decision and that I wasn't just acting on impulse.

So I shared with Mom the feeling I'd had when I charged the catcher during the baseball tournament. "Mom, I don't remember ever in my life having a feeling like when I ran around third base and collided with the catcher on my way home."

I struggled with the idea of having nothing to do while all my friends were at football practice. From the time I was a kid, I hadn't liked being alone. Who would I hang around with if all my friends were hanging out with their football buddies?

Coach Santopadre needed to know my decision. "Coach," I said when he answered the phone, "I'm going to play football."

"That's great, Thomas!"

"Just so that you know, I'm a baseball player playing football to keep in shape."

"Any way you want to see it is fine with me."

The first day of practice, Coach Santopadre was visibly happy that I was joining my friends to play freshmen football. He embraced me, slapped me on the back and said, "Welcome to the team, Thomas!"

I thought I would easily slip into football practice, just as easily as I'd slipped into playing most sports.

But my friends had all been practicing for weeks already. I didn't know any of the plays; I barely even knew any of the positions.

"Fullback line up over here."

"Go through the A-Hole."

"Go through the 2-Hole."

"Go through the 4-Hole."

"Even numbers are on this side of the line of scrimmage."

"Odd numbers are on that side."

What in the world was everyone talking about? They were speaking a language I didn't understand.

And the target kept moving. How can you tell me that the A-Hole is over here, but when that guy moves I can't see the hole any more. Where is the hole?

I was really confused.

About the only thing I had going for me was that as a freshman, I was about the biggest kid on the team. At six feet and one hundred ninety pounds, I was hard to push around.

I was physically bigger than most guys on the team.

I could hit and I could run. Collisions no longer worried me. In fact, now I welcomed them. All those years as a younger child on the playground, at the park, I got into trouble for using my physical size to gain an advantage in any game we were playing. Here on the football field, I could be as physical as I wanted. In fact, I was encouraged to be even more physical than I was initially.

No one judged my antics. My rants. My rages. My trash talking.

Trash talking was encouraged.

Competition was welcomed.

It got so that every time I got on the football field I wanted to scream out loud for the pure joy and happiness I felt playing tackle football.

Ninth grade was sure to be an excellent year.

CHAPTER 18

Comfortable At Being Uncomfortable

The first day of my freshman year arrived and Mom drove me over to the high school. As we approached, it horrified me at how uncool it would look for Mom to drop me off right in front of the school, hugging and kissing me in front of everyone.

"Mom, drop me off here."

"Thomas, I can take you all the way to the front of the school."

"No, Mom. It's OK. Just drop me here." I gave her a quick kiss and hug and slammed the door on her voice telling me to have a good day.

Approaching the front of the school, I was both excited and apprehensive. I caught sight of some of the guys on the freshman football team and I ran to catch up with them.

It felt good to be associated with a group.

I was a football player . . . until spring, when I'd be a baseball player again. No one pushes a football player into anyone's locker. No one was going to call me names. No, my only fear about high school lay behind all the doors that opened to the corridors currently filled with hundreds of students.

Inside the classroom was my nemesis.

Learning.

My best report card in eighth grade was a 2.3 average.

What if high school work was harder?

What if I can't maintain a 2.0? I wouldn't be able to play football, that's for sure.

I knew something had to change about how I applied myself in the classroom. Fortunately for me that change came in the form of competition.

Joey was a buddy on my football team. After one math class where I didn't understand the assignment, I jogged to catch up to him in the hallway. "Hey, Joey. Can you help me understand what's going on in math class?"

"Sure." As we suited up for football practice, Joey quizzed me on some of the concepts from math class. After practice he said, "Thomas, do you want to hang out and do homework together? I can help you some more."

Doing homework together was a new concept for me, but it couldn't hurt. Our nightly homework sessions became our pattern. At least at first.

But I was still having trouble with some of the math homework. Mom had suggested that I go in to school early and ask my math teacher for some help. As I entered the math room, I saw Joey was already there, ahead of me, talking to the math teacher.

I listened in on what he was teaching Joey, and fortunately it answered my math questions too. Later that day as we suited up for football practice I asked Joey, "Why were you in Mr. Belson's class so early?"

"I needed help. The only way I can get help is going in before school. I can't get it after school because of practice."

"Oh, you sly dog, you. You were going to sit there and leave me in the dark and not tell me?" Joey didn't hear me say this as he was already jogging out to the football field. It didn't matter, I had his number now.

The next morning, I showed up even earlier than Joey did. I had Mr. Belson all to myself for a private tutoring session for almost twenty minutes before Joey got there.

Good old competition.

We were soon showing up at the math room door before Mr. Belson got there. He'd grin, unlock the door and beckon us in for our tutoring session before school started.

Even our math homework was a competition.

At one point we were doing matrix problems and Mr. Belson would give us about a hundred problems every night. Joey and I would sit together after football practice and fly through our homework to see who could get done the fastest.

"How many did you do?"

"Did you get them right?"

"You going in early tomorrow?"

Once my competitive drive gets going, I really begin to perform. As long as there was a challenge, I wanted to compete. It became about finishing more than Joey, and getting more right than he did. Working through my freshman math class with both Mr. Belson and Joey and I finally started to see results because I was applying myself.

As I'd learned in sports, it's not enough to just show up.

You have to actually do the work.

The other benefit to getting extra help before school and working with Joey after school was that during football practice my mind was free and clear. I wasn't constantly worrying about whether I had my assignments done which worked perfectly because on the field, my mind had to be on football.

꧁ ꧂

As the season progressed, I began to realize that football was huge at Vacaville High and people started recognizing me around the school. My freshman teachers would say, "Thomas, I heard you had a great game last night." P.E. coaches, varsity coaches, varsity athletes were all telling me I'd played a great game. I was doing a good job.

And we were.

We were undefeated until midway through the season when we lost the game right at the very end.

I watched it happen, and it was as if nothing I did could change the outcome.

As a team, we weren't able to finish.

We had been winning, but we lost the game in the last minutes because we had run out of steam.

Coach Santopadre was the one who convinced me to join freshman football even though he coached varsity football, but it was his oldest son who actually coached us as freshmen.

I remember watching young Coach Santopadre as an athlete and thinking that he had to be the most competitive person I'd ever see nplay ball.

As we slunk, defeated, off the field, I could see young Coach Santopadre's face. He held in his anger and frustration because he didn't want to let loose in front of all the parents and kids in the stands behind him.

"Tonight, I want you to understand what it means to finish."

Uh-oh. We all looked at each other. This was our first loss, so it was the first time we really got a tongue-lashing.

He went on, "I'm going to teach you how to finish. This will help you build up your endurance. Your stamina. Your mental toughness. Tonight I want every last one of you to go home and do one hundred push-ups!"

We all groaned. We were defeated. Exhausted. We had played the most challenging game so far of the season, and the last thing we wanted to do was go home and work out some more.

But I did it.

I went home and started my push-ups. I was tired already from the game. My arms were exhausted. So I broke it down into ten sets of ten push-ups. I didn't go to bed until I finished all of my pushups because that is what Coach said to do.

The whole time I did my push-ups in front of my mom I worried about what she was thinking.

Was she going to laugh at me?

I was afraid she would think I was weird or crazy for working out in front of the television with her. Eventually I realized that my worries about my mom were just that. Worries. My objections were all in my head. She had none at all. As always, Mom fully supported anything I chose to do.

The next day I met up with my teammates. We started going around the circle of us asking, "How many did you do?"

"I did thirty."

"Forty."

"I didn't do them all, I was too tired."

"Fifty."

"Seventy-five."

I was shocked. No one but me had done all one hundred push-ups.

That is when I had a personal epiphany.

In order to get what I wanted, I had to be willing to do what others weren't willing to do.

Listening to my teammates, I realized that they were too lazy to complete the one hundred push-ups.

As a result, I started to do more. Each week I added on twenty more daily push-ups. One hundred twenty, one hundred forty, one hundred sixty.

I knew I had to do this.

Some days I would wake up with my arms so tired I could hardly wash my hair. I realized that if I really wanted to be better than everyone else, I had to do more than they did.

I had learned what it meant to finish.

CHAPTER 19

Report Card

Report card time. Mine arrived on a Friday and I heard Mom call out from the kitchen to me in the living room, "Thomas, your report card is here."

In all my years as a student, starting in kindergarten, I had never brought home a report card that pleased Mom. Report card day was never one of my favorites. It was a day that resonated with my mom and grandparents chiding me, pushing me to improve.

"You can do better, Thomas."

"Not again!"

"Oh Thomas, what happened?"

Mom was still in the kitchen and so far hadn't said anything. I knew what was coming, and braced myself for it.

When she spoke, her words surprised me, "Thomas, whose report card is this?"

I thought to myself, hurray, they sent the wrong report card. I was safe until Monday. But, just to make her happy, I joined Mom in the kitchen.

"What do you mean?" I asked.

Without speaking, Mom handed me the report card and I saw three B's and three A's.

I knew that a 4.0 meant all A's. So three B's and three A's was a 3.5.

And a 3.5 was really good.

I checked the name on the report card. It said Thomas. R. Williams.

It was my report card. I had never gotten such good grades before.

Mom shouted and hugged me so hard I thought she might never let go.

I felt so proud of myself, and yet I hadn't been worrying about grades, I had just started challenging myself both in sports and in school, competing with myself and with my teammates. Whatever they did, I did it and then some.

That was part of my formula to success. My past no longer haunted my future.

Mom's next words scared me. "Thomas, now that you've set the bar up this high, you have to do it again."

What did she mean, do it again?

What if it was just luck?

What if I couldn't do it again?

My success scared me because I was afraid it really was just beginner's luck. So to be doubly sure, I increased my efforts in school.

I couldn't let Mom down.

More to the point, I wouldn't let myself down.

⁕⁕⁕

When baseball season arrived, I noticed something about myself.

I had become complacent.

I was that player where everything came easy, so I didn't have to try. Baseball had always come pretty naturally to me, so I didn't feel I had to put in the extra effort, the extra practice. I felt I knew everything already.

Last fall in football, I had to stay after practice because there were things about football that I didn't understand.

I had to practice the technique of leverage in being lower than your opponent, and rolling your hips when you make a tackle, and running my feet constantly through a tackle. I had never learned those skills, so I had to put in a lot of extra effort.

For football, I didn't mind.

On the positive side, I was in spectacular shape for baseball, just as Coach Santopadre had suggested I would be.

Midway through the season it hit me.

I no longer loved baseball.

Baseball didn't drive me as hard as football did.

I played just fine and performed well. But I didn't have the desire to be the best player. Baseball no longer challenged me.

I'd become infatuated with another love, and her name was football.

She yelled at me, made me sore, but I loved it.

I had become a football player who was just playing baseball to stay in shape.

My freshman year I finished with a grade point average of 3.3. I knew that Coach Santopadre would have no trouble at all persuading me to return as a JV football player.

CHAPTER 20

Friday Nights Under The Lights

After Coach Santopadre had begun calling me the summer before ninth grade, I became used to taking calls from him on the phone.

He became a natural mentor to me.

When the phone rang now, I was excited to answer. "Hi, Coach."

"Hey there, Thomas. The other coaches and I have been talking about you and your football abilities. We've decided that we're going to bump you up to varsity football this year." From the expectant pause on his end of the phone, I could tell Coach expected me to be stoked. I expected to play junior varsity with the rest of my friends.

To play varsity in my sophomore year, what an amazing opportunity.

But I knew to be careful what I asked for. It all sounded great on the phone in the air-conditioned room. Immediately I visualized every part of being a varsity football player, the Friday night football games, the letterman jacket, the crowds.

All of it.

To play varsity meant that the attention was going to be on a bigger, grander stage than I had experienced last year playing freshman football.

"Sure, Coach." What else could I say? I tried to act like this was no big deal.

I wanted to sound cool, not like some cornball.

Friday night varsity football games made up a lot of my memories as a kid. Everyone from town gathered at the stadium of the school, under the lights, in the stands.

Teachers.

Parents.

Students.

In those days I'd marveled at the games. As a kid when the "National Anthem" played I would close my eyes, my right hand over my heart and imagined myself as one of those players. When the words "home of the brave" played, each player raised their helmet. That was a Bulldog tradition, and I held onto that image inside of my mind.

This time, I would be on the field holding up my helmet.

Then articles in the newspaper would appear the following morning, articles of community acknowledgment of what those players had done on the field on Friday night. According to Jason across the street, you know you've made it when your picture appeared on the front of the paper. He would ask me, "How many fronts can you get by the time you graduate from high school?"

Now Coach had chosen me to be one of those players.

I allowed my daydreams to carry me, but once I started looking out for the guys I'd be playing with on varsity, a little niggle of fear ignited in my gut. These were the guys I'd been watching play on Friday nights. I saw them at practice and in my mind, I was still just a lowly freshman. These were the guys I'd read about in the papers and now I was supposed be playing alongside them.

Suddenly I felt outclassed.

During weight training fear started pressing into my heart. I allowed all kinds of negative thoughts into my mind and my battle to be on varsity was almost lost before it had even begun.

What if I couldn't play as well as those guys?

The whole concept of moving directly from freshman football to varsity was filled with minefields. Here I was, fifteen years old and I was going shoulder to shoulder with the seventeen and eighteen-year-old players of my school.

These guys were the size of grown men. I still saw myself as just a little boy.

Me taking a spot on varsity meant that there was one upperclassman who did not get a spot. I didn't want to be the reason someone else didn't play.

The "what ifs" started:

What if the guys on the team hated me?

What if I didn't know the plays well enough?

What if I just wasn't good enough to be on varsity?

The more I thought about it, the more I began to realize that Coach had made a mistake. I figured it was time to fix this problem before it got any bigger.

I wasn't admitting to myself that I liked being a big fish in a small pond. Now I would be expected to compete at the varsity level, to strive in ways I had never done before. Before this I had played well on my freshman football team, coasting, relying on my natural talent. I was comfortable there. I was good there. To be moved to varsity made me think that I was being given something I hadn't earned yet.

Standing in line to get my issued equipment the first day of practice, I saw the guys I'd played with last year. I'd already been through the process before. Instead of going last as a freshman player the way I had the year before, as a varsity player I went first.

My friends on JV waited to take their turn, and all of them were watching me. I assumed a lot of them were wondering. Why does he get to go first? Why Thomas?

I couldn't give them a good enough answer.

Just as painfully as they felt it, I understood the distance between my friends and me was growing. How could I make them understand this wasn't my fault?

I hadn't asked to be put on varsity.

I wanted to be on JV with them.

After I got my equipment, I hustled over to where the head coach was giving his pep talk. All of us were gathered, varsity, JV, and freshman players. He gave us his take on what the season meant to Vacaville High, how we earned our victories in the "dog days" of training camp.

Then we were off.

Freshman players went to their field.

JV players went to their field.

And varsity used the field we had just huddled up on.

As I watched my friends and former teammates walk away from me heading to the next field, at what should have been the coolest moment of my life, I felt a stab of guilt at my success and their apparent loss. The only reason I even wanted to play football in the first place was walking away from me. My friends were leaving me behind to play with the strangers I only knew as the upperclassmen on varsity.

I had everything I needed to succeed. I had the size and basic skills. What I lacked was the mental toughness and heart to see the entire effort through. It didn't take a genius to know that I was going to get run over by the guys on varsity. Sure enough, the first day of summer practice, I got creamed. Topping six feet and weighing in at over two hundred pounds, that wasn't an easy task.

I needed the heart of a lion. What I brought with me was the heart of a mouse.

After the first day of practice, I went home complaining. "Mom, would you call Coach and tell him that you don't want me playing varsity football this year?"

Not only did I believe I was incompetent, but I just wasn't good enough to play varsity. For the first time ever, I wanted to run away from my problems in the sports arena.

Mom looked at me for a moment, then shook her head. "Thomas, I'm not going to do that. Stop being scared. You're just as big as those other kids. Just as strong. And you're just as fast."

Mom was right.

But she didn't know about my fear. I was afraid to play varsity football. After I'd been knocked down over and over during practice, I decided I would just force my coaches to move me back down to JV. After a hit, I didn't get up with any kind of fight in me. I spent an entire week just going through the motions, sure that they would notice I didn't have what it took to play varsity.

I was overmatched, overpowered, and didn't have the talent it took to be on varsity so soon.

It was time to talk to Coach and get him to move me back to JV football, so I waited until after he'd finished chatting with the other coaches after practice. All the other players had dispersed after the "one-two-three Bulldogs!" that we always said when we were done. It was fall, and the sun very low on the horizon, almost dinnertime.

"Hey, Coach. You got a minute?"

"Sure, Thomas. For you, I have all the time in the world."

Not quite sure how to broach the subject, I cleverly decided to go with the idea that I wasn't an asset to the varsity team. "I kind of think that maybe we jumped the gun putting me on varsity this year."

Coach just looked at me, waiting for me to go on, a grin on his face. It never mattered what problem I brought to Coach, his attitude was everything's OK. I think he already knew where the conversation was going, but I couldn't read his eyes.

"I don't think I'm understanding the plays that well."

Coach just nodded, not saying anything.

He wanted more? I didn't understand. I wasn't that good. I wasn't sure of the plays. I was getting run over on the field. And over time I'd come to realize that the real reason I really enjoyed playing football was because I was able to spend time with my friends. I knew I should have been proud to be on varsity, but I wanted to go back to where I was comfortable. I'd had so much success as a freshman that having to work hard to compete to just be good enough was a lot of work. More than I wanted to put in right now. My friends weren't even on this team.

On Junior Varsity, I could play well enough that no one would be able to see through my facade. And, I was good enough that I didn't have to work hard to keep pace.

On varsity if I messed up one play, the entire town would think I was a failure. I wasn't sure I could handle that. I had never experienced criticism in sports before. I had never been coached to handle it. I never needed it before.

Coach listened until I finally ran out of words.

We both looked at each other for a beat.

Was he mad?

Was he disappointed?

I honestly couldn't tell.

The Coach nodded and said, "You bring up a lot of good points, Thomas."

Hurray! He was going to send me back to down to JV to play football with my friends, to a place I felt most comfortable.

"So, let's just see how it goes."

See how it goes? What was he talking about?

"Just play it out. We'll reevaluate in a couple weeks and make a decision before the first game."

Hadn't he been listening?

I'd visualized this conversation going a whole lot different. I figured he'd listen to me and then say, "Sure Thomas, I understand. No problem. Go back to JV and then you can come up to varsity next year."

But that's not what happened.

Coach left me on varsity.

He totally outplayed me in that skirmish.

CHAPTER 21

F-E-A-R

The lesson I learned was that the number one killer of all dreams is fear. F - E - A - R. I knew that people talked about me athletically. I was the kid who had literally shot out of the canon.

Who is he?

I figured everyone was thinking to themselves, he must be good. And they would want to go to the game on Friday night to see the team and this new kid.

This time the new kid was me. And I wasn't feeling so confident. I knew I had taken a spot that could have been filled by an upper classman, whether a junior or a senior. I was new. Younger. People had to be wondering, why is this sophomore playing varsity? What's the deal with him? The thought followed me like a dark cloud. I didn't have an answer for them. People more powerful than I had decided this was where I needed to be. I sure hoped they were right.

I was terrified. Our first game imprinted itself on my mind because even though I'd been practicing with the varsity team, I still didn't feel like I was really part of the team.

Our first game against the Napa team, Vintage, was a home game, and it arrived a lot sooner than I really wanted it to. My first time on the field in front of the school and the town of Vacaville gave me stage-fright. I could hardly sleep the whole week before the game, my nightmares traumatizing me. More what-if questions erupted.

What if everyone made fun of me because I wasn't good enough to play on the varsity field?

What if I miss the tackle that loses the game for us?

What will my team think?

What will the town think?

It's one thing to mess up in practice, and I'd been doing that pretty regularly. But it was an entirely different thing to mess up in front of everyone under the Friday night lights.

Every morning the entire week before the game I met with the coach for an hour and reviewed plays. The instant I left the room, I immediately forgot everything I learned. I feared I would blow it for everyone. Right before the game I asked a couple of my teammates, "Do you think we're gonna win?"

Who would ask that?

"Do you think they're big?"

My teammates knew I was afraid.

"What's the matter? You scared?"

I'd already come to the realization that I enjoyed tackling. I LOVED the physical contact of football. That wasn't what scared me about playing varsity. What I did worry was that the guys on the opposing team would be bigger than the guys on my team I'd been practicing against. I'd worked myself into a state of incompetence. In my mind I wouldn't be good enough. I wouldn't accomplish the task.

Walking out onto the field, I took one look at the opposing team and freaked out. For the past month I'd been tackling the guys on my team. I knew their size. Their speed. Their agility. When I assessed our opponents that night I broke out into a cold sweat.

Look at those giants!

I could smell how mean and crazy they were.

My position was linebacker.

Basically, I tackle the man with the ball.

As play proceeded that night, I didn't even want to be a linebacker any more. Being a punter sounded pretty appealing. I could be out there in front of the crowd, wear a jersey, get all the glory and accolades without any effort.

No such luck. So I simplified my job.

Find the football.

Tackle the player who had the ball.

Later, when I reflected on my performance, I thought to myself that I'd done OK. But in reality, I'd gotten yelled at badly by the defensive coordinator. Mom was in the stands and heard it. That meant everyone else heard it as well. Mom said if he ever yelled at me like that again he'd get a visit from her. There was a camcorder the coaches utilized to record every play of the game. When we watched the recording afterward it made me want to crawl into a hole. But I couldn't say they were wrong. The evidence was there in the recording.

I had messed up.

What I feared the most is exactly what happened.

I couldn't admit to anyone, player or coach, that I had closed my eyes on every tackle. I played with my head down. Bad technique.

I was scared.

The swagger I had during freshman football wasn't anywhere to be found on the varsity field. I'd met a new level of competition.

That night I hoped rather than knew that I'd be successful. The problem with hoping is that it means there's a chance of failure, of not completing the task.

I wanted to be in a position of knowing, knowing that I could complete the task.

Because when you know, well you just know.

When you hope, there's a lot of uncertainty.

The one good thing about that first game was that it was over in the blink of an eye.

Everything happened so fast.

It seemed like the guy with the ball was there, and then in less than a blink of an eye, he was gone.

I had no time to think about my plan of attack. I could only react.

Later, when I reviewed my performance of that game, I was ashamed. The coaches were watching the same film, they're SURE to send me back down to JV. I'm a liability.

But I didn't want to go.

NOW I wanted to stay, if only to redeem myself.

Initially I hadn't trusted myself. I played that first game hoping to get by without making a mistake. I played most of the game just guessing.

And when you play to not make a mistake, you miss the opportunity to be great.

I was afraid to fail, so I failed to succeed.

I didn't take risks because I feared the tongue-lashing I got from the coaches when I made a mistake. I feared the embarrassment of being chewed out in front of the school, the town.

Fears holds you back from being great.

As my sophomore year went on, I became a little more comfortable playing on Varsity. I eventually became one of the guys, but my first year was not stellar.

What I feared the most is what happened.

⁓◦⊙◦⊙◦⁓

"Thomas," Coach stopped me as I walked by his office.

"Hey, Coach. What's up?"

"How are you feeling about the season?"

Hmmm. That was a loaded question. I was finally feeling comfortable though I still missed my friends who were playing on JV. On the positive side, I was holding my own and identifying myself as a varsity player.

"I feel good."

"Good. Just wanted to check in with you." He smiled his knowing smile.

As I stood up to leave something caught the corner of my eye. I just glanced and saw a kid's name on an envelope. Who was it addressed to? There were letters from various universities around the country sitting on Coach's desk. They were from CAL, Notre Dame, University of Texas, LSU, Alabama, and Stanford. I looked closer, figuring that they would be addressed to Coach, but they weren't.

They were addressed to players on my team.

Why would universities around the country be sending letters to my teammates?

Not wanting to display my ignorance to Coach, I sought out one of the upper classmen on my team who had several letters addressed to him.

"Hey Josh, there are letters in Coach's office for you."

He looked at me, giving a slight shrug of one shoulder, "Yeah. Those are just a bunch of recruiting letters."

"What are recruiting letters?"

"During your junior year, college scouts go out and find players who can move onto the next level for a scholarship at their school."

Josh's body language indicated boredom, as if the idea of the schools sending him recruiting letters was a burden he didn't want to deal with. Yeah, just another letter. Or maybe he figured everyone knew about the letters and he didn't want to spend his time to educate me.

Too bad for him. I had eight minutes between classes to get my questions answered, so I pressed him for information.

CHAPTER 22

Aha Moment – Ignition!

As questions peppered out of my mouth, Josh looked at me astounded. For me, that was the moment everything clicked.

I had to know how to get colleges and universities to write to me!

My desire to be in the spotlight reignited and somehow I just knew this was my next goal. How do I get some of those recruiting letters for myself?

To have letters arrive at the high school from coaches around the country was definitely the next step in my journey for validation. Coach had just asked me how I was feeling about the season and while deep inside I still doubted my abilities, the rest of me loved being a varsity football player.

Playing varsity football and getting noticed, that would be my ticket out of Vacaville!

"How do you get them to write to you? Just play hard?"

Josh, leaned his back against the lockers, giving me the impression that everyone should already know this information. I didn't care. I was learning that what I don't know can hold me back from getting what I want.

"Thomas, there's nothing you can do. They have to come out and recruit you."

"How?"

"You play hard. You ball out."

I could do that.

After my first varsity game, I no longer wanted to be sent back to JV and my natural competitiveness helped me to play all out.

"What if I mess up when someone's in the stands?"

"Who cares? Quit being afraid of messing up. Just play the game."

Josh's words opened my mind to the thing that might have been holding me back. I'd been playing it safe, trying so hard to not mess up that I wasn't playing all out. My focus had to change. I had to play the game with one goal in mind, to succeed. My vision of success had to be far greater than my fear of failure.

This I could do.

Then Josh went on, "It's not enough that you play hard. You have to keep a certain grade point average. You have to go through the NCAA Clearing House. You have to get a good enough score on the SAT. And you have to be a role model in the community."

I listened intently.

I had already decided to play harder on the field. And my additional effort in math had brought my GPA up. I knew I could handle that.

But I didn't understand what the NCAA Clearing House was, and not one single person had yet mentioned me taking the SAT exam.

I headed to class, my head filled with even more questions.

Once I started asking my classmates what they knew about taking the SAT, I was shocked to discover that any student planning on going to college or university had to take it. I used to think that only kids who intended to go to a prestigious college like Stanford, Harvard, or Yale had to take the SAT. Because that wasn't my plan, I hadn't even worried about the SAT. Now I had no idea if this was hard to do or not.

As usual, I went to visit Coach Santopadre to ask him for direction. If there was a way to becoming a pro athlete, Coach would be there to guide me.

"What's up with this NCAA Clearing House, and the SAT test? How do I do these things?"

Coach smiled a little as if he knew I'd finally been hooked. "So you're serious now?"

I nodded. Yes. I was serious. I had to get out of Vacaville, and an athletic scholarship looked like the only way it was going to happen for me.

"Well, Thomas, you're a sophomore and all these steps have to be completed by the time you graduate, otherwise it will be too late."

Too late?

No way was that happening.

"So what do I need to do?"

"OK. Let's do it," Coach said. "I'll go and check with the counselor to see if you're taking the classes you need. I'll see you at practice."

Now I had a set goal and time was working against me, not for me. I had only two and a half years left in my entire high school career and if I was going to do something, I had to do it now.

Right here.

Right now.

Later that day, Coach walked up to me on the football field and said, "I checked on your classes and you're in all the classes you need to be in. Now we just have to get you ready for the SAT."

ふみ ゑみ

I had heard the SAT was a long test and you had to study for it.

Math.

English.

Reading.

Reading? I'd never read a book cover to cover. That was the monster under the bed for me. The more I thought about it, the more I began freaking out. I'd finally learned how to do better in my schoolwork. Wasn't that good enough?

Apparently not.

This was another lesson for me to understand, Just showing up and doing well wasn't good enough.

I went home that night and talked to Mom. Taking the SAT test really had me worried and so I asked what she suggested.

"Thomas, any time you have trouble with something, you need to ask for help."

No kidding.

I knew it was going to take a whole lot more than just getting me a little help. I never did well on tests like the SAT. Anytime I ever had to test with the rest of my class, I experienced such a high level of anxiety that I believed I was going to pass out right there at my desk.

To be honest, I thought I was stupid.

Dumb.

A failure.

For just a moment, I had serious doubts about whether I was ever going to make it big as a football player, all because I wasn't a very good test taker.

But I'd worked too hard to give up my dream.

I had all the information.

I had the roadmap on how to get there.

Now I had to figure out how I was going to pass the SAT.

Mom came through and found a tutor for the SAT exam. Every Saturday we'd drive to a library in Davis where I would meet with my tutor for three hours and he would drill me, give me formulas, visualizations, anything and everything I could possibly use to be successful on the exam.

On the way home from each session Mom turned to me and asked, "What did you learn today?"

And I just stared at her blankly.

I didn't know.

I couldn't remember a thing he'd taught me.

One day I made a joke of it, "Mom, I learned what my issue is."

She looked at me, curious to see what I had discovered.

Without hesitation, I said to her, "I'm stupid!"

Anytime I couldn't talk my way out of something, I relied on humor. But the look on Mom's face told me she didn't think this was funny.

And I got it.

She was paying her hard-earned money to help me succeed and I wasn't scoring well enough on the practice tests to demonstrate that I was making any improvement.

This discouraged me.

I wanted to do well on the SAT.

I had to do well on the SAT.

I also wanted Mom to know she wasn't wasting her time driving me to my tutoring sessions or wasting her money paying my tutor.

Yet the harder I tried, the worse my scores seemed to be.

At first I would compare my practice test results with my friends, but they were scoring very high on the practice tests without using a tutor.

Reality set in for me and I figured I would never make it.

Even though my grades in school were solid and I was an above average athlete on the field, I was terrified that none of it would matter because of the low score I knew I would get on the SAT.

Nothing I did helped me.

I had to figure out an alternative because if I didn't pass the SAT my dream was crushed.

Then I learned two key facts. First, I learned the minimum score I had to get on the SAT to have "passed" it. Second, I had more than one chance to take the test. If I didn't get the minimum score, I would have to take the test again. Second chances were always good.

The rest of my sophomore year I continued to work as hard as I'd learned to do in my freshman year.

I made some changes in my social life too. I had a core group of friends, Robbie, Zach, and Mike. If those three guys weren't going to be at an activity, I didn't go either. In that way I distanced myself from some of my other friends who weren't taking school and my football efforts as seriously as I did. That was OK. They had different goals and dreams than I did. Different agendas.

On the weekends, when everyone else was hanging out and partying, I was playing "Beat the Clock" by working out harder, studying more. I did not go out after football games because I thought if I still had energy to go out after a football game that meant I hadn't given my all during the game. My friends continued to call me. "Hey Thomas! Where are you? We're going to hang out at the party at so-and-so's house."

But I never went. I knew there would be drinking, drugs, even sex. And I didn't want to pollute my body with any of that.

I had to keep my eye on the prize. In every decision I made; from the number of pushups and situps I made myself do to the kind of food I put into my body.

Everything was a part of the bigger picture, the goal, the dream to become a professional athlete.

Everything I did either helped me or hurt me.

Desperate times, desperate measures.

Scholastically, school was very difficult for me. The only way I pulled my grade point average up was by really applying myself to my studies. And I pulled my grade point average up because I now knew I had to be a well-rounded person. I couldn't possibly get into college without good grades.

I discovered something in high school. We become what we repeatedly do. I used to try to justify things, especially early in my life. I'd give excuses for any of my failings.

Now, I knew that if I don't follow the rules of the game, I'm out. Getting to the NFL was the dream. If improving my grades was part of the path, I had to get my grades up. If passing the SAT was a rule for my goal, then I had to pass the SAT.

In order to succeed in the game, I had to first know the rules and then follow the rules.

That made perfect sense to me.

You have to stay in bounds on a football field. You have to stay within the lines on a baseball field.

So, you better stay inside the lines of the game of life if you want to succeed. I used all the obstacles and the way I had learned to overcome them in sports to help me in life.

I may never be the best student of Vacaville High, but I was certainly one of the most dedicated.

For a long time I had searched for the secret to success.

There was no secret.

Just hard work.

Every single thing I wanted to do, there was a price to pay. My price meant I avoided partying, drinking, staying away from the curiosity of women at the time. They were not going anywhere. They were there before me and they would be there long after I was gone.

I decided to give up what I wanted now for what I wanted in the future.

CHAPTER 23

How Do I Pass The SAT?

My linebacker coach, Coach Green, was a giant of a man. He stood six feet six inches tall and he had to weigh about four hundred pounds.

At practice he yelled at the top of his lungs in the deepest voice I had ever heard in my life making me feel like an absolute midget.

But one of the most important things I learned from Coach Green was that he never used cuss words and he demanded that we not use them either.

If we cussed, we had to run to the furthest part of the field and pick a leaf from the ivy on the fence there and run all the way back.

By the time I graduated I had quite a collection of ivy leaves.

Coach Green had been the object of my youthful adoration from the time I was a kid going to the Friday night football games. I would watch that giant of a man with the entire team huddled around him. Now, I was one of those guys huddled around him. His pregame and half-time speeches would have us ready to run through a brick wall for him.

Another dream erupted during that time; I wanted to have that same ability. To have the power to get others to believe in an almost supernatural ability just because of the words I said to them.

Most importantly, Coach Green taught me about integrity. He was a man who truly practiced what he preached. He believed in my abilities on the field even when I couldn't believe in them on my own.

He taught me that real men don't do what the rest of the crowd is doing just because. Real men do the right thing. No matter what the cost of doing the right thing is.

✸❧ ❧✸

Weeks flew by, summer came and went. Before I knew it, my junior year began. The looming SAT continued to give me nightmares. I decided to take the test as early as my high school held the test just so that I could get it out of the way.

Continuing to prepare for the test, I asked other kids about their experiences. Todd was the smartest kid in my school and I asked him what he had gotten on his SAT. It sounded really high. His answer really didn't help me much and part of me wished I hadn't asked him.

The day of the test arrived.

All my preparation was over. All the studying I could do had been done. It was time to face my greatest fear. Prior to this, my greatest fear had been joining the varsity football team in my sophomore year. The SAT scared me even more than that.

I shuffled into the room with my pencils. A fellow athlete from another school sat down next to me and told me to keep my paper uncovered during the test so he could look at my paper.

What a knucklehead!

He had no clue about my problem taking standardized tests. And he apparently didn't know that we got different test booklets to prevent that kind of cheating.

I didn't know what to tell the kid. I knew how afraid I was to take the test, but here was a guy who was even less prepared than I was.

It was going to be a long day.

I started the test strong, but it didn't take very long before my frustration, my fear, and my self-doubt took over.

Here I have to be one hundred percent truthful.

I gave up on myself.

There were points during the test I felt like I couldn't even read the question, so I just filled in some of the answer bubbles so I could hurry up and escape.

The relief I felt when I finally handed in my answer sheet almost made my knees buckle. Taking the SAT was harder than any game I have ever played in my life. It totally drained me.

Once the test was over, I put it out of my mind. I was thrilled that I didn't have to keep taking the practice tests, and doing the drills, and memorizing formulas to things I didn't understand. Instead, I focused on what I could do something about, and that was I continued to work really hard on my school work.

Soon the SAT results came in.

I scored ten points over the minimum score I needed to get in order to pass the test and meet the NCAA Clearing House requirements.

I had done it!

I had faced my worst fear and survived.

After the SAT, I believed I could face anything.

CHAPTER 24

My Only Competition

There was no doubt about it, my junior year of high school was the most important year of my life. This is what I had been dreaming about and it had finally arrived.

It was the year that college scouts and coaches would travel to Vacaville High to watch us play football.

I'd done everything Coach Santopadre had told me to do as part of the recruiting process in preparation for this year.

Time for me, Thomas R. Williams, to be noticed on the football field.

I projected supreme confidence in my athletic abilities to everyone I talked to; coaches, teammates, friends, and teachers.

But deep inside, I was afraid. My confidence was a mask, deep down inside I was extremely nervous. Riding the bus on the way to our first high school game I sat next to Coach Pop. Pop helped me out after practice every single day and knew me as well as anyone. He looked at me and asked, "Are you ready?"

"I'm nervous."

Pop looked at me and smiled. "Nervous? Nervous for what? The only reason you should be nervous is lack of preparation. You've worked your tail off. It's OK to be anxious, which you probably are, but never be nervous."

The power of words affects what we say and think making it more likely to happen. Pop's words affected me profoundly that day and every game I played in the future. Rather than describe the physical feelings I was having as being nervous, I began to view them as anticipation, excitement. The feelings register the same inside your body, but what you call them makes a difference in the outcome.

In my mind, Vacaville paled in comparison to larger towns. What if it was too small for the college scouts and coaches to find me? What if no one ever came to watch me play? What if my dazzling performance on the football field went by unremarked, unnoticed, never seen? I desperately wanted to be chosen. But what if they never saw me? What would I do?

Fortunately, my coaches had been through the process of attracting regional and national attention for their athletes in various sports. Coach Tom Zunino said, "Thomas, if you're good enough, they will find you."

I took his words to heart. They calmed me down and allowed me to continue to focus on my next step. I knew I was good enough. Fear and excitement feel the same, the difference lay in the conversation I was having in my mind.

"Thanks, Coach. I needed to hear that."

"Thomas, only worry about the things you can control. Whatever you can't control, let them go."

"Like what?"

"You can't control how many scouts or coaches come to your games. But you can control how you play the game every time you're on the field. You can control your effort; in practice and during the game. You can't control how many will come to the school looking to meet you, but you can control how well you do your schoolwork and by how you contribute to your family and the community."

Not many high school juniors I knew were able to do as coach suggested. They worried about all kinds of things and as I listened to them, I realized they were wasting time and energy worrying about things they couldn't control.

Maybe Coach was right.

My effort was fully within my control, so the summer going into my junior year I seriously intensified my workouts. I did double workout days to be physically prepared for the test of playing varsity football my junior year, playing for the coaches who were looking for my kind of talent to represent their colleges and universities.

My double day workout started in the morning. I went to Gold's Gym with Kyle and another friend named Mike where we did cardio and then worked out on the weight machines. Then I would work out in the afternoon with my team where we would run, lift weights, and perform football-specific drills. We only had two hours to get everything in at practice, and once our time was up, it was up. Because I didn't feel this was enough preparation, I picked up the habit of doing more than the team was doing in order to become an elite athlete. I had to go above and beyond. I slept better at night knowing that I had done everything possible that day to ensure my future.

Each day, I woke up and did it again.

For me this effectively silenced the voices of doubt that sometimes found their way into my head; voices that said, Thomas you can't do this, you're not good enough. What makes you think you're so special? What makes you think you're going to be any different from your father? Your family? Why do you think you should be the first one in your family to go to college?

The only way to silence the voices was to work harder and harder. By the end of the day I was so exhausted from my rigorous workouts that I slept harder than ever before. Believe me, when you work as hard as I did and sleep as deeply, you aren't going to hear the voices anymore.

Keeping my motivation for those double workouts each day was a huge challenge, because I'd discovered that no one else wanted to do the same things I was doing. During the summertime, a lot of my friends would sleep in, waking up only when their eyes open. They might play video games until it was time to show up to the mandatory team workouts. Then there were the parties after the workouts.

I knew that my future could only be different if I behaved differently than everyone else. I secretly invented a workout buddy, an imaginary friend like you might have as a kid.

Only my imaginary friend kept me honest.

He was me. Only better.

Always with me, he could run faster, do more sit-ups, push harder. If I did ten reps, he did eleven. If I did twelve, he did thirteen. If we were at practice and I ran wind-sprints or worked out after practice, he always did more of them, always faster and harder than I did. He always kept me on my toes.

It was as if I wanted to feel as if I never did enough, and this imaginary workout partner pushed me to do more every time. Never relaxing my guard. There was no room for complacency because my imaginary workout partner always showed me up.

And I hated to lose.

That person slept with me, did homework with me, ate at the dinner table with me. He became like the twin brother or the older brother who was always better and received more applause and praise than I ever did. I don't know if I invented this imaginary competitor because I was an only child, but I do know I created this competitor to keep me always striving. I'd learned years before in baseball that when you think you're plenty good enough, that's when you lose your drive. The instant you lose your passion, it's almost like death. Your edge is what keeps you alive and relevant in the game of sports. It was my makeup, my identity.

There is always someone else out there who is better than you in every way. It wasn't enough to challenge myself by just being better than the best guy on my team. I had to be better than everyone else in the county, in California, in the entire country.

I even allowed my imaginary competitor to force me to do better at my schoolwork. If I were watching TV, my imaginary competitor sat right beside me, but rather than watching what was on the television screen, he studied, writing out the paper due at the end of the week or doing the math problems in preparation for the upcoming test.

If he was studying, I studied.

I developed a mantra by which I measured my choices: If it isn't helping me, it is hurting me.

Simple. Black and white.

Decision making became ultra-simplified.

I had already spent way too much of my life ignoring the consequences of my actions; from fighting on the playground to not listening to my teachers in class when I was in elementary school. I knew better now. All those hours and days I'd been sent away from the classroom were hours and days I'd never get back, and the lessons taught at those moments were lessons I never learned.

In order to never make that mistake again, I evaluated everything based on whether it helped me or hurt me. If I had to study, I knew that the longer I put it off, the more tired I would be. Being tired and doing homework was not a good mix, so I usually chose to get my schoolwork done first. Deciding to get the homework done allowed me to go to class the next day feeling confident from all the preparation and work I had put in the night before. My class participation improved and as a result my grades continued to improve.

☙ ❧

My mantra also helped me make choices about friends and the activities we did together. I started to notice that more and more of my friends thought it was cool to smoke weed, drink, and party. Add girls to the mix and it was about as explosive as a Molotov cocktail.

I had heard so many horror stories about guys who had all the ability, all the talent, all the intelligence they needed to make it big. They were destined to become the next "All American" hero. But they let drugs, alcohol, or girls pull them away from their dream.

For me, all that had to stay right where it was.

I knew that in ten, twenty, even thirty years, those couches filled with partying people would still be sitting there, those beer bottles still in the cooler, those same joints passing from hand to hand, only everyone in the picture would be ten, twenty, thirty years older.

And they will have accomplished nothing.

If what I'm doing today isn't going to get me closer to my dream, it had to go.

Many of my friends didn't understand my mindset. I wanted to tell them, if I have to cut you out of my life, I'm sorry, it's nothing personal, it's strictly business.

My clock was ticking, time growing shorter and shorter. What time I had left had to be filled with the activities that would put me closer to my dream.

CHAPTER 25

Temptations And Distractions

People accused me of being a robot with how dedicated I became to football. What they didn't seem to understand was that football was for me what their partying lifestyle was to them. I didn't feel like I was missing out on anything.

Football for me was my girlfriend, my attraction, my addiction. Food for my soul, my spirit.

As my mistress, football fed every part of me. And sure, I was tempted by girls, but it always came back to the question, is she going to help me understand offense or defense better? No? And she's not helping me to get faster, stronger, and bigger? She's not going to help me with my grades. Sorry. The girl's gotta go.

It was Coach Santopadre who helped me understand how falling in love with a girl could jeopardize my entire athletic future. He asked me to make him one promise and that was to not fall in love.

He'd seen me starting to have some puppy-love feelings for one of the girls. We'd talk between passing periods. Sometimes we'd see each other after the games.

He watched and he worried. One day after practice he came up to me and said, "Thomas, make me one promise. Promise me that you will not fall in love while you're in high school."

"What do you mean?" Who was he kidding? Who was I kidding? I knew what he meant, but didn't want to admit it.

"The last thing you need is to get involved with a girl."

"Coach, it's nothing serious."

"So tell me what happens when it does get serious. What happens when you get a scholarship to go to a different state and she isn't going to go to the same school you're at?"

"I'll be fine, Coach."

"What happens when you get a little homesick? You're missing your girlfriend and you lose your focus?"

I knew where he was going with that line of questioning and while I didn't like it, I knew he was right.

"Thomas, I've seen it over and over again. A talented athlete goes away to college on an athletic scholarship, comes back because he misses his girl and his scholarship is gone. Then a few weeks or months later, they break up. Now he has nothing. No girl. No future as an athlete. And no more free education."

I shook my head. "Not going to happen to me, Coach."

"Make sure it doesn't."

And he was right. The feelings of puppy-love I'd been feeling were beginning to distract me. I was spending a lot of time convincing myself that we'd both go to the same school, that we'd both get our dream, that everything would be perfect for both of us.

But all it would take is for one thing to go wrong and everything would explode for both of us.

So my almost-girlfriend and I stopped hanging out together because football was my true love, calling me back and reminding me of my dream.

Football was my one true love and any girl would have gotten tired of waiting for my obsession to pass.

I loved football so much that I was perfectly willing to forgo the experiences of high school in order to realize my dream. I wasn't going to be one of those guys who talks about all the things I could have done if only I'd just tried harder.

I had to try harder today.

Not tomorrow.

Not next year.

I'd watched my mom work way too hard to get me where I was. If I stopped trying now, it would be the same as saying that all her effort just didn't matter. So my dream was not only for me, but for my mom as well.

Without all Mom's effort, I wouldn't be where I am today, so every choice I made must include taking her into consideration.

⚬⚬ ⚬⚬

We played our second game of the season in my junior year against a team from Napa and I managed a huge hit against the quarterback during the second quarter. While the play was underway, my entire focus was on hitting this guy.

After I hit him, I heard a huge roar of approval from the crowd.

Every defensive player's dream rose to heaven on that sound from the stands.

I read about my exploits in Saturday's paper. Sunday my friends talked endlessly about the play. My coaches congratulated me, talked about it, analyzed it.

On Monday when I walked between my third period and fourth period classes, I heard someone yell, "Thomas!"

I turned around to see who called out my name. Mr. Lopez, the tennis coach and Spanish teacher stood there.

"Yeah?" Usually when a teacher calls my name in the hallway, I cringed. So many years of my youth were spent making teachers angry with me that I still preferred to not really have teachers notice me.

But Mr. Lopez smiled and yelled down the hall, "That was a hell of a hit on Friday!"

I grinned, waved my hand in the air in thanks because not only did I get the admiration from a teacher I'd never had a class with but the hallway was filled with students who heard his words. They, too, began to gather around like I was the next new star. Which is exactly what I had been looking for my entire life, someone who didn't have to tell me that I was good. Here was someone totally outside my circle taking the time to recognize me.

Mr. Lopez continued, "I can't wait to come and see you next week."

I had a fan.

He was coming to the football game next Friday just to watch me play. It put pressure on me to put on a show again under the lights on Friday nights. Where there was one fan, there were bound to be more. This was my reminder to never become complacent. If I didn't feel like practicing hard on Tuesday, I'd think back and realize that there would be another fan coming to see me play on Friday night. A fan I couldn't let down.

I knew everyone coming to the game came to watch the team.

The Bulldogs.

Now, I knew people were coming to watch me play.

Mr. Lopez had thought about my play all weekend long in order to tell me on Monday morning. To be on someone's mind for the whole weekend fueled me to play even better.

And soon every time I was in the hallway during passing period, fellow students would comment on my playing abilities, creating a buzz at Vacaville High.

"Thomas, great game."

"Hey, great play Friday night."

"How many yards are you going to rush this week?"

"How many tackles will you have?

I didn't need to party.

I didn't need to drink or take drugs.

The kind of recognition I was finally getting for playing football was so much more powerful than any drink or drug known to man.

CHAPTER 26

Special Delivery

S oon I started getting even more attention. I sat in Algebra II doing my homework during quiet time. Mr. Ruiz allowed for students to start their homework and ask questions if they needed help.

As everyone worked quietly, the door to the room opened. As in every classroom in the country, all eyes in the room raised to see who was at the door.

A teacher's aide handed Mr. Ruiz a note. He read the note, stood up and announced, "Thomas, Coach Jones wants to see you immediately."

I gathered my books, looking calm on the outside, but inside my mind raced. Why did Coach want to see me now? Football season had ended and baseball season was beginning to heat up. I hadn't gotten into any kind of trouble.

As I usually did, I walked into his office, knocking on the door as I entered the room. I saw Coach Jones was talking with a stranger.

"Oh, I'm sorry. I didn't mean to interrupt, I'll come back later."

"No, no, Thomas. You're not interrupting. Come on in."

Coach turned to the man in his office who stood up to greet me. "Thomas, I want you to meet the coach from Louisiana State University."

LSU?

"Nice to meet you." At least my manners came to my rescue because my brain felt short-circuited. A coach from LSU was here? To see me?

As strange as it sounds, the whole time I talked with the LSU coach, my mind asked me questions I couldn't answer.

And the questions had nothing to do with football, and everything to do with the father that had been virtually missing from my life for many years.

Here was a man who had traveled all the way from Louisiana just to see me.

Why couldn't my dad do the same thing? I was a part of him. He wouldn't come see me, but this man who didn't even know me was spending time and money to travel to meet me.

I wanted to say, Dad, look at me. An LSU coach has come to watch me play football. Now people are starting to come meet me and want to pay for me to be a student athlete at their university.

I kept refocusing my mind on the conversation with Coach Jones and the stranger from LSU.

"Thomas, we just finished watching your highlight film."

Just the previous year I'd wanted to get a letter of interest the way my friend, Josh, had gotten. No letters yet, but having a man get on a plane to come and see me, that showed serious intent.

And serious intent stood before me in the form of the man in his LSU polo shirt and his purple and yellow hat who continued talking. I didn't even process his words. My first coach visit and I was ecstatic. For me, this was my Heisman trophy. Being pulled out of class, getting special treatment. I struggled to focus on what Coach and the LSU coach were saying.

"We know that you have what it takes to play at the next level."

My dream of becoming a professional athlete was coming closer and closer. I could just feel the excitement mounting almost on a daily basis. Those words had a surreal quality about them.

Had it really even happened? I'd invented an imaginary workout partner, maybe I'd invented the coach from LSU.

No.

I knew it happened.

Finally, my dream was beginning to open up in front of me.

I walked back to my classroom on cloud nine. When I entered the room, everyone crowded around me. They could tell by the smile on my face that nothing bad had happened to have been called out of the classroom.

"Who did you see?"

"What happened?"

I smiled and said, "A coach from LSU came to talk to me about maybe playing there after I graduate."

"Wow!"

"Congrats, man!"

"That's amazing!"

And it was amazing. I could hardly wait to get home to tell my mom. All her sacrifices over the years to help me reach this level of competitive sports were finally paying off.

Every little boy wants to say, "Hey Dad! Look what happened." I wanted to share this news with a man. With my dad. But he still wasn't around, and that dimmed my joy just a bit. I finally felt as if I was doing something Dad would be proud of, but I couldn't share it with him.

The class bell rang and I could hardly wait to find my friends to tell them about my visitor from Louisiana. As I walked down the hallway, one of the senior varsity football players from my team stopped me.

"Hi Tony." I couldn't help but grin from ear to ear. I was sure he'd heard the news by now and was coming to congratulate me.

"I heard a coach from LSU was here to see you today."

"Yeah. Isn't that amazing?" I couldn't contain my enthusiasm. This was the highlight of my life, everything I've been working toward.

Tony shook his head, frowning. "What are they here to see you for? There's no way you're going to LSU."

I stared at Tony. "What do you mean?"

"You can't play Division One ball."

My mind reeled.

In the space of a split-second I went from being so happy and proud of my accomplishment to being filled with fear and self-doubt. When I shook the hand of the man who had traveled all the way from Louisiana to meet me I'd felt that I was at the pinnacle of my sports career. His very presence in my school, asking to see me, was proof that I was good enough.

"Whatever, man," I said with a laugh. I didn't know what else to say to Tony. I didn't want to confront him, but I didn't want to stay there talking to him right then because he was trying to kill my vibe.

Then it hit me.

Tony was a dream stealer.

He wasn't getting coaches coming to see him. He was already a senior and if he hadn't generated interest as a junior, he was the one who wasn't able to play Division One ball.

Tony might have been a smart kid and he played OK football. But in that instant I hated him for trying to steal my dream away from me.

This wasn't his dream.

It was mine.

And in that instant, I resolved to never let anyone divert me from my goal. Not with their words, their actions, or their thoughts.

What they thought about me was their business. Not mine.

I reminded myself, if it doesn't help me, it hurts me.

Tony's words weren't helping me, so I discarded them. The only thing that mattered was that I knew the path I was taking and I wouldn't stray from it.

All my life I'd taken opinions of other people and turned them into a dare for myself. My thoughts pumped up my determination to show people who didn't believe in me that I was capable of far more than they thought. When my teachers would say that I would never amount to anything, I would think, oh yeah? Well let's just see who's laughing at the end.

After LSU came to visit me at school, it was as if the flood gates opened and day after day I would be called out of class to meet with another coach.

On top of the visits from coaches, the letters started coming. My first letter was from USC, my first choice if anyone asked where I wanted to go. When Coach handed me the letter with the USC letterhead on it, I felt like I was going to explode.

I took the letter home and showed it to Mom who was only just beginning to see that there was quite a buzz about her son. Maybe she'd had so much disappointment in her life she didn't want to get too excited only to have her hopes dashed again. She was very happy for me, but I sensed some reservation in her.

I took the letter from USC into my bedroom.

What should I do with it?

No way was it going in a drawer. I looked around my room and then tacked the letter onto the wall. Directly in the middle, eye-level so I would see it every day. It would remind me to never quit, never let up on the pursuit of my dream.

Every evening I'd share with Mom about my day. I'd been such a trial to her that even though she had proof of my intentions, like my 3.5 report card my freshman year, it still wasn't quite sinking in.

"What do you mean someone came to see you at school today?"

"It was a coach, Mom. They might want me to play for their school after I graduate?"

Once it finally sunk in that there were people who really were watching my football career, Mom got right down to business. "What do we need to do?"

"Relax, Mom! Everything's going just the way it's supposed to."

And in that moment, the radiance of her smile made every single push-up, every single extra sprint, every snide comment from a teacher telling me I'd amount to nothing, all of it became worth it.

Just as I couldn't wait to get back on the football after Mr. Lopez had commented on my play the previous week, I could hardly wait to make Mom smile again. One of the greatest benefits to finally getting noticed was that Mom was finally getting noticed too. She was the one who made sure I had every opportunity available to me. She had cleaned houses for other people in order to support us. She went back to school to get a better job just so that she could keep me in sports and equipment for my various athletic activities. She had scrimped and saved in order to make a life for the two of us. Deep down, I knew she had done it for me.

Now that I was being actively recruited, the coaches and scouts talked to Mom too. When I was done talking to one of them on the phone, they asked to speak to Mom. As those men recruited me, they wanted to know what kind of home environment I came from, wanting to know about their new recruits. Who are we really recruiting? They liked what they saw because anytime they called, they asked how Mom was doing. It was not to butter me up. They really liked her.

Finally, my hero was getting some good attention. We were on this journey together and I wanted her to enjoy the celebration as much as I did.

For me, I never got tired of the letters or the calls out of the classroom to meet yet another coach. One day it was LSU, another day it was Washington, then Texas, Notre Dame, Nebraska. And on and on.

Sometimes I would be called out of class to meet the visitors, other times Coach Santopadre would bring them around campus and when he caught sight of me, he would stop me and introduce me to that day's visitor. It was as if I were a celebrity and my fellow students were the paparazzi, they would gather around and watch as I'd meet yet another coach from a college from around the country.

Eventually, I escorted the visiting coaches around campus and introduce them to my teachers and friends myself. I wanted all my teachers to know that I was worthy of their attention. When I came in and spent extra time asking questions about the day's work in the classroom that I wanted them to understand exactly how serious I was about going to college. Maybe I hoped that they would give me the benefit of the doubt that if my grades were teetering between a lower or a higher grade, they might just give me the higher grade.

Because the thing is, you can't just play football. You have to be able to be the best football player and get good grades.

Without the grades, there was no football.

I began to realize that teachers are people too, and if they don't see results from their efforts, they become jaded. They start to think the worst of their students. In elementary and middle school, I'd certainly done everything in my power to make them think that way and probably deserved every bad or negative thought my teachers had about me.

One day, I dream of going back to some of those teachers and apologizing to the ones I'd given the hardest time to. But even more importantly, to thank the teachers who actually saw through my acting out and realized that there was just a kid inside my body who didn't know how to get his message across.

Those teachers are the ones who saved me because they changed my life. I wouldn't have been able to walk around campus with football coaches from literally every major college or university in the country without the effort they had put into my education.

They believed in me when I didn't.

CHAPTER 27

"May I Have Your Autograph?"

With my junior year at Vacaville High behind me the sound of the ticking clock controlled my every breath.

One more year of high school.

One year left for my dream to become a reality.

I'd managed to get plenty of scholarship offers from colleges and universities around the country and I knew I had to make a decision this year as to where I would go.

I focused on football, doing everything necessary to maintain my skills, my momentum, and interest in my abilities. There was a persistent, irritating fear deep inside of me, fed by the uncertainty I wouldn't be good enough.

Mom understood how I felt and decided to become my workout partner. That summer before my senior year, we both went to the high school and worked out together. We ran laps around track. Then we would run up and down the bleachers.

Mom surprised me in how hard she worked and how well she kept up with me. It reminded me how hard she had worked when she had gone back to school to get her medical assisting degree.

Mom never quit. Which meant I couldn't quit either.

Once Mom was done with her workout, I continued, because I wasn't finished with my program yet. She took the stopwatch and timed me through all my drills and football exercises.

"Work harder, Thomas."

"You have five more seconds."

"You have five more reps."

"No, you are not finished yet."

Her words encouraged me to work harder and harder. When I thought I had hit the wall and could do no more, I would put my hands on the top of my thighs as I bent over, gasping for breath.

"Thomas, what are you doing down there?"

Trying to lift my head, I replied, "I'm resting."

"Never bend over. Ever!"

What was she talking about?

I was done.

I was tired.

Then I learned Mom's number one rule, "Don't even think you're tired."

And she was right.

The instant I allowed myself to think I was tired, I was tired.

In that way, Mom kept me going even when I was ready to quit. Some nights we worked past sunset and the janitor at the school would turn on the lights at the field so that we could finish our workout.

All around me were kids going to the pool, going on summer vacation. My summer was the same as all the years before. I had to get things done before I ran out of time.

Some people asked why I didn't ever develop the same symptoms of "senioritis" that other kids did. My one honest answer: I was too tired. I didn't have time to think about messing around.

I'd worked so long and hard on my dream and my senior year was the last chance I had to make it happen. In my mind, time still ticked away.

◦◦◦

There comes a time when too much of a good thing might be too much. Two weeks before the beginning of the most important football season of my life, I woke up with a sore ankle. I knew it had happened during one of my workouts and rather than listening to my body, I decided to push through the pain. I'd shaken off enough sore and stiff muscles in my athletic career, and this seemed to be a similar injury.

My body had healed before, it would do it again. I just needed to work out, get the blood and sweat flowing.

This time, my body betrayed me. Two days before I reported to training camp of my senior season, my ankle throbbed to the point I could not walk.

Terror overcame me.

What if I couldn't play this season? How could I continue to pursue my dream if I couldn't walk?

So far, I had not told my coaches, but I knew that I had to report my injury.

I limped into the first day of training camp and we all knew that in order to overcome my injury, we had to take things day by day. I figured I would just do some of the exercises, I knew I could favor my ankle.

They sidelined me.

"Complete rest," they said.

I participated in training camp from the bench, watching my teammates as they sweated through their football exercises and drills. I had to wait it out. And yet I could continue to work on my craft mentally. I took mental reps. I watched the films. I lifted weights. I just couldn't play during practice. Fortunately I had learned to focus on what I could do, yet not playing made me miserable.

As if my misery weren't enough, we had reporters coming by practice. They wanted to get a general sense of how the team was shaping up for the upcoming football season.

Now I wasn't just miserable. I was terrified.

I didn't know if I would be able to play this year or not, but I wanted to keep my injury as quiet as possible. After all the hard work and preparation I'd put into getting to this point in my athletic career, I couldn't afford to be seen on the sidelines, or worse, have my picture taken on the sidelines.

The instant I knew a reporter was coming, I hid. News about my injury could spread like wildfire to college coaches and my chances of playing for one of the college teams could disappear.

Fortunately, my injury improved with the enforced inactivity and after two weeks I rejoined my teammates on the field.

During my time on the sidelines I developed a much greater appreciation for the game I played. It was absolutely a privilege to play football. After my two weeks of rest, I was back in the game and worked as hard as I could to make up for lost time.

I intended to play all out during my senior football season.

 oༀ ༀo

Other people noticed me, people who were not involved with football. I needed an elective for my senior year so Coach Santopadre made me his teacher's assistant. One day I went down to the front office to have his mail sent off. While I was there, Ms. Montoya, one of the secretaries handed me a piece of paper and a pen.

I looked at her. "What's this for?"

She smiled and said, "I'd like to get your autograph before you become a pro ball player."

I smiled as I signed my name to her piece of paper, but inside I was flustered.

I had been dreaming about becoming a professional athlete. From the third grade I'd been asking God almost every night to help me become a professional athlete.

And here was someone who had watched me grow up in the halls of Vacaville High. She saw my potential.

Sure, I had been dreaming this.

But a part of me didn't really believe it could happen.

Yet here was someone who recognized my intent and believed in me.

As I walked back to Coach Santopadre's office I realized that secretary saw something special, something great in me.

Wow!

And yet, why not me? Why not a kid from Vacaville?

It was certainly what I wanted and had been working for, but as I signed my first autograph, I realized that notoriety can be a double-edged sword.

Sure, on the one hand you get all the attention, the crowds, the lights, the publicity.

On the flip side I feared letting her down, of letting everyone down.

Just as I'd done last year, I had to choose to accept or reject thoughts based on whether they helped or hurt me.

The fear of failure would hurt me.

In my black and white view of the world, I had to believe I would succeed. In order to do that, I had to believe in myself. I had to see myself becoming that professional athlete right now, even before it actually happened.

Looking back, I saw how people like Ms. Montoya had helped me.

Mentors.

Teachers.

Coaches.

Friends.

Everyone I met had some kind of influence on me and how I pursued my dream.

CHAPTER 28

Go With Your Gut

One of the first turning points of my senior year was Senior Night, the last home game of the season and all the current seniors were recognized because they would be moving on the next year. Senior Day marked their very last appearance on the home field as a high school athlete.

Senior Night was a huge event and created a great deal of anxiety for me. All through my youth years I'd attended the football games at Vacaville, I'd watched from the stands as the seniors of each year were recognized with their parents.

On Senior Night you walk out with your parents. Your mom and your dad. They walk you from the goalpost to the fifty-yard line. You get your picture taken and then you go to the sideline.

That event was no surprise to me, but as it approached I began to have a lot of anxiety about it.

Who would I choose to walk with me?

Obviously my mom would walk out with me. But who else?

Sure, I had a biological father and while I'd only spent one year living with him after my parents divorced, he was still my father. But my only contact with him consisted of a couple of brief visits and the occasional phone call.

I had a number of other men who had stood in my dad's place and provided me with a lot of guidance both in sports and in life.

As the event approached, I got on the phone with my dad and the level and depth of my emotion startled me. This was the first time I ever allowed my father in, asking for something I needed. Never before had I told him how I felt. I didn't tell him my fears. I was afraid he would eventually leave again. This time I showed vulnerability. Every week my teammates walk off the field with their dads who are carrying their gear.

And not once had my dad been here.

I wanted approval, recognition from the one man who hadn't given it to me. Just once I wanted him to say, "Good job, Son."

It had taken me years, but I finally asked him, "Dad, where have you been? Why have you never seen me play football?"

"T, you know it's a long way for me to come."

"Dad, men I have never met in my life have made time to get on a plane and travel out here to meet me. And my own dad has never seen me play football."

I don't think he understood exactly how important football was to me.

"OK, T. I'll come and see your next game."

"Really?"

"Really. Let me know the dates and I'll be there."

After that call, we spent a little more time on the phone as I tried to get Dad caught up on what I had been going through with the recruiting process. I'd tell him what schools I was thinking about attending and which coaches had come by the house that week. Sometimes I wondered if he thought I was stringing him along, but I tried to get him caught up on the last couple years and how important each of the events had been.

"What's this Senior Night about?"

"It's where the parents of the athletes walk them out on the field."

"Do you want me to be there for that?"

Perhaps I'd been so afraid he'd say no that I hadn't asked him before. More accurately, it was my way of protecting myself against additional disappointment.

"Dad, I just want you to come out and watch me play." To my horror, I started to get really emotional. I wasn't quite crying on the phone, but he could hear that I was tearing up.

"If it's that important to you, T, I'll come. And I'll be there for Senior Night too."

The excitement I felt equaled the feelings I had the year I went out to live with him when I was in second grade. My dad would finally, finally see me play football.

He would see me doing the thing I love most on this earth. I could introduce him to my coaches, my teammates, my friends. I wanted him to see what he had been missing.

I would no longer feel the responsibility of trying to make it clear over the phone what my life was like. He would be here. He would witness it firsthand.

Coach Santopadre was happy when I told him of my decision. "Wow, Thomas. That's great. I can't wait to meet him."

And then my thoughts turned to the man who had shaped much of my athletic career.

Ron.

Mom and Ron had been broken up for some time, but I couldn't ignore the impact Ron had had on my life. I even asked what Coach Santopadre thought about asking Ron to walk me out on Senior Night.

"That's a good idea too."

Coach never told me what I should do. But as I used him as a sounding board, something became very clear to me.

Dad didn't deserve to be my partner as I walked out on the field on Senior Night. He wasn't the one who taught me how to play ball.

He didn't encourage me when I was down and frustrated about my abilities.

The man I called "dad" gave me life. But he hadn't been there for all the things a dad does for a son. A dad is someone who teaches their son how to ride a bike. He helps you figure out what to say to a girl when you want to ask her out. A dad is the one there to teach you how to tie your tie on prom night.

Dad hadn't been there for any of that.

What was I supposed to feel for this man who gave me life and yet had been largely absent from my life ever since? A handful of visits and sporadic phone calls did not make up for the hole his absence made in my life. I had a father, but I didn't have a Dad. I now understood the difference between a father and a dad.

The day Dad came out to see my football game filled me with conflicting emotions. He let me drive his rental car yet couldn't help himself from correcting my driving. In his mind I was still six years old.

"Check your blinker."

"Look over your shoulder."

"Put your blinker on, watch out for that car."

"Watch out for that pedestrian."

I just shook my head at each correction. I'd been driving for two years by this time and I felt mom had done a good job teaching me.

In my mind I was thinking, don't try to be a daddy to me now. You missed that opportunity.

I realized what I wanted was for him to be more of a friend than a father. I needed a friend. I'd made it this far without a father. It was fabulous for him to meet my coaches and my teammates and see how my efforts impacted the team. As the day of the game progressed, I sensed he realized he'd been missing out on a lot of things in my life.

Sadly, everything he missed was gone forever. With each story people told him about my efforts as a freshman, as a sophomore, and as a junior, I could see his sadness. He listened to people tell him what a great son he had. I didn't have to point out the hefty price he'd paid for not being present in my life.

After the game Dad said, "Good job, Son." The words warmed me because we'd lost the game.

I'd played well, but I realized I didn't want his admiration as much as I wanted him to understand how the experiences on the field brought me so much joy. I didn't know how to tell him that, I hoped he would see it in the way I played.

As he was heading back to the airport, he talked about Senior Night and my only response to him was, "I'll call you and let you know."

I never called him.

My feelings were so horribly conflicted, but when I made the decision to not call him, I had already decided that Ron deserved to walk out with me on Senior Night.

Mom and I had some trouble sorting that out because she was seeing another guy and didn't want to cause any problems.

The more I thought about it, the more it became clear to me that Ron needed to be the one to walk me out on the field on Senior Night. To the world, on that one night, he would be my dad. He would be the one I recognized as having "raised" me as a man.

Mom resisted, "Thomas, this is going to be really awkward. The family will be there. Bob will be there. Could you have Papa walk you out?"

I knew she was trying to make this better for everyone, but as much as I loved my grandfather, Ron was still the one who had played ball with me for hours in the front yard, who had watched game after game of baseball with me, teaching me terminology and plays. Ron had sparked my interest in sports, never judged me, and always worked with me on becoming a better man.

But this event, Senior Night, was my night. I made one of the biggest decisions of my life to that point and stood up for what I felt was right.

"I'm sorry, Mom, but I want Ron to be there too. I understand this might make you feel uncomfortable, but Ron will walk with me because he is the one I look toward as a father figure."

I know she understood, even though it made her feel uncomfortable.

During lunch the next week I went to Ron's jewelry shop to visit as I had done even after he and Mom had broken up. "Ron, Senior Night is coming."

"That will be a big night for you, Thomas."

"I would be really honored if you would consider walking out with me that night."

Ron stared at me, the moment as surreal for him as it was for me, but I think he finally realized just how much his involvement in my life had meant to me.

With a huge smile on his face Ron said, "Are you kidding me? I would love to!" That told me all I need to know. He was absolutely thrilled to be asked, which speaks volumes to his character. He didn't expect my request, but it pleased him more than anything else I could have done. His reward had been watching me turn my life around, not to take credit for my accomplishments.

On Senior Night, Ron had his name announced along with mine and my mom's. We took separate pictures because there was a limit to how uncomfortable I was willing to make Mom. I had a picture taken on the fifty yard line of Mom and me. Then I had a picture of Ron and me which he later hung in his jewelry shop.

That was a decision I never regretted. I knew I had the opportunity to do the right thing and I didn't want to live with regret years down the road.

CHAPTER 29

Imagine: 5 Years From Now . . .

During the second semester of my senior year, my economics instructor, Ms. Dahl, gave us a very interesting assignment.

Define the Roadmap of Your Life.

We were to diagram what our future would look like in five years.

The assignment was to answer the question, where will I be in five years?

I've had a vision for myself that remained virtually unchanged for years. Not only had I dreamed of it, but I was well on my way to making my dream become reality.

Once Ms. Dahl gave us the assignment, I began to map out my plan. Unlike a number of my classmates, I welcomed the opportunity to establish the steps required to become a professional athlete.

What college do you plan to attend?

What will your profession be?

How much education is required?

What will this cost?

What will your annual salary be?

A number of my classmates intended to be lawyers, doctors, teachers, vets, accountants, etc. I was the only choosing to be a professional athlete.

The assignment was a good one. I had no idea what I could expect to make. I had just operated on the premise that it would be my way out of Vacaville. I knew I had to go to college, but everything else required some research.

As I researched, I learned that I had to attend at least three years of college in order to be eligible to go into the NFL draft.

I decided that my professional team would be the Miami Dolphins. The rookie salary was $220,000. I chose the car I would drive. I selected my apartment, its size and how it would be furnished.

I really got into the assignment. I fully entered the shoes of this guy who planned to be a professional football player. It occurred to me that people would think that I was some kind of a joke. How many people actually make it all the way to becoming a professional athlete? The real numbers shocked me. It is less than one percent in the entire world.

But I knew myself and I had no intention of giving up until I got what I wanted.

On presentation day, I was totally prepared to share what I intended to do with my classmates. Many of them knew I was addicted to football, but most of them didn't realize that I fully intended to go pro and that I had mapped out my plan. Some of them might laugh at me, but I didn't care. I knew exactly how I wanted my life to turn out.

When my turn came to present, I felt so liberated to share my journey. I went through my entire presentation and then as required I asked if there were any questions. Some of the students snickered under their breath thinking that I had chosen the "easiest" job so I didn't have to put any effort into my presentation. From those knuckleheads I answered questions like:

"How much will you make?"

"What car will you drive?"

"What number do you want to wear?"

But as I answered their questions and gave them more information than they expected they began to realize I was totally serious about my project. Then they began to ask better questions.

"Why did you choose to play for that team?"

"Why did you choose to go to that college?"

"How long will it take for you to achieve your goal?

For the most part, my classmates seemed interested, engaged, and accepting of my presentation.

All but one girl. She asked, "Thomas, what if you get hurt? What is your backup plan going to be?

I don't know why I took that as a challenge, but I didn't have a backup plan. I couldn't afford a backup plan.

I asked her, "What occupation did you choose for the rest of your life?"

"I'm going to be an attorney."

"So if you get hurt and can't do that job, or if you never pass the bar then you have to have a backup plan too, don't you? I guess I'm going to do the same thing you will. I'll figure it out if it happens." She looked stunned. I guess she didn't have a backup plan either. Her dream and aspirations were the same to her as mine were to me. If she didn't need a backup plan, neither did I. She might have been a bit offended, me suggesting she might not pass the bar exam, but it was no more offensive than her thinking I couldn't achieve my dream.

The more time I spent thinking about something else, figuring out what I would do if my dream didn't come true was taking energy and momentum away from what I was planning to do right now.

I chose to not have a backup plan.

It wasn't because I was lazy or inadequate. It was due to my laser focus on becoming a professional athlete. I didn't care how long it took. It absolutely never entered my mind to put limitations on my goal.

Whatever it took, I would do it.

That was the first time I had ever verbalized my dreams to people other than my teammates. I was vulnerable and completely exposed by sharing my dream with people who didn't have the same belief that I did.

I received an A on the assignment. The teacher also wrote in her comments "Thomas, Great Job! Go get your DREAM!"

∽ೲ ೲ∽

National Signing Day is the day high school athletes sign on with the school of their choice. It is the day every single high school athlete across the country waits for. All the sacrifice, all the commitment, all the determination over the years culminates in that one single moment when you put your name on the dotted line and commit yourself for the next four to five years.

For me, National Signing Day topped Senior Night. As much as I looked forward to graduation, I was pretty sure it would be even bigger than that. I knew I would graduate. Every step forward I took as an athlete had been mirrored in my scholastic efforts as well. Not one teacher at Vacaville High doubted my efforts in their classrooms by the time I hit my senior year.

After Senior Night when I'd asked Ron to accompany Mom and me on the field, I continued to think back on all that man had done for me. And I wanted Ron to be part of the continuing process on the road to my dream.

No one was surprised that I chose the University of Southern California, USC. It had been my first choice from the very beginning and that my first letter was from USC might have been a coincidence, but to me that didn't matter.

I had chosen USC long ago.

But today was the day I would legally commit to that university and I wanted the people who had supported all my efforts along the way to be there. Obviously Coach Santopadre would be present; I would be signing at his house. No doubt Mom would join me. Without her, I might very well be the drug dealer that Mr. Truman had predicted, or I'd be dead.

But Ron was my wild card.

Ron is the one who spent hours talking to me about sports. He spent hours on weekend afternoons helping me perfect my pitching and batting abilities. He took me in when I returned from living with my dad and treated me with love, respect, and compassion.

Not once did he try to be my dad. But what he did was even better. He did all the things a dad would do for his kid without being my dad. It didn't matter that I was the half-black son of his girlfriend. What mattered was that I was a kid who needed some guidance and he'd given it to me. He'd taken a chance with a woman who had a child from a previous relationship and he had treated me like family.

This wasn't a topic I ever discussed with anyone. It meant so much to me as the kid who constantly wondered why his own dad couldn't be there for him to teach him the ways of the world.

After having Ron accompany me on Senior Night, I never had a single doubt that he should accompany me on signing day.

My problem was that while he and Mom had been very close for a long time, they had broken up. One thing about Mom, you knew where you stood with her. Breaking up with Ron meant no Ron in her life.

I'd managed to get her to go along with my Senior Night plan, but I wasn't so sure about National Signing Day.

That didn't give me much choice. I wanted the three most important people in my life to be there that day: Mom, Ron, and Coach Santopadre. Ron and Coach were on board. But Mom presented a bit of a problem.

I resorted to a bit of subterfuge. I told Ron to come and pick Mom and me up the morning of National Signing Day. But I didn't tell Mom Ron was coming because I feared that she would say she wouldn't go, or worse, she would force me to choose between the two of them, which I didn't want to do.

The plan was to have breakfast with Mom, head over to Coach Santopadre's house to sign the paper and fax it to USC. We didn't have a fax machine, so signing at Coach's house made perfect sense.

Breakfast went as planned, though my stomach was full of butterflies, wondering if USC was the right decision for me, as well as worrying what Mom would do when she found out what I'd done to trick her. She was dressed and ready to go, doing the dishes when she looked out the window.

"What is Ron doing here?"

At first I was silent. I hoped she would just go along with things.

Mom turned from the window and looked dead at me. That did not bode well. "Thomas?"

"Mom, this seems like the only way I can tell Ron thank you for everything he's done for me."

Mom continued to stare at me, then threw down the dish towel and went into her bedroom.

Filled with anxiety I waited to see what she decided to do. When the door opened and I saw she had changed back into her pajamas, I had my answer. I'd lived with her long enough to know that trying to change her mind would never work.

I walked out to Ron's truck. He'd had the presence of mind to just wait and see how things played out inside the house. With a heavy heart I climbed inside Ron's truck and said, "She's not coming."

"You still want me to go?"

"Yes." And I did. I was just so sorry that Mom refused to come too. That moment represented the biggest achievement of my life and while Ron and Coach were there to witness it, I felt so sad that

Mom refused to be there too. It certainly wasn't the way I'd pictured it before going to sleep the night before.

We drove to Coach's house to sign the paper and take photos of the moment. I faked a big smile because my biggest support, my strongest "why" hadn't come to join in the celebration.

CHAPTER 30

I Can ~ I Will ~ I Did

My name was announced. "Thomas Ray Williams, Jr." Those were the words I had waited a lifetime to hear. The screams from the audience told me that plenty of my friends and family members had been waiting to hear them too.

Today was graduation day.

My entire family was there, even family I had never met before had flown into town for this moment.

When the announcer pronounced those words I walked across the stage to accept my high school diploma with so many conflicting emotions doing battle inside of me.

To Mom, without you, I would never have reached this pinnacle of my youth.

To Mr. Truman, you were wrong man. I'm still here and I'm not a drug dealer.

To Ron, thank you for helping me to become the man I am today.

To Dad, you gave me life and a yearning for something more than I had.

To Coach Santopadre, the fact that you never gave up on me taught me untold perseverance.

To my teachers, you never know when what you say or do will affect even the most resistant student.

As I accepted my diploma, I thought my heart would burst with pride at my accomplishment. I was a student athlete, heading to the University of Southern California and I had done it on my own merit. I'd learned how to study, how to pass the standardized test requirement to get in, and still be the very best athlete I knew how to be.

Could life get any better?

There really was no feeling like hearing your name as you cross the stage at your graduation.

After the surreal experience of the graduation ceremony, my family joined me on the field for pictures and I smiled so much that my big cheeks began to cramp.

At one point, Mom and I were the only ones in the photos. I squeezed her so tight and whispered in her ear, "We DID it!" And that moment remains etched in my memory. As a boy, I hugged my mother, thinking how much stronger and bigger she was than I. Now, at two inches over six feet and two-hundred-twenty pounds I was finally the man who could protect her.

We both knew that this moment might not have happened. There were plenty of times I could have failed, but I didn't.

In the moments of that embrace we celebrated our greatest triumph, the greatest accomplishment Mom and I ever had together. We had defied every single odd that had been set before us; from her a single white woman raising a biracial child in a predominantly white community to me being accepted by USC on a full athletic scholarship.

It had been a team effort, and I loved how it felt. I could tell by her smiles that she shared my emotions.

Back at Mom's house, we gathered. I knew that this would be the last time I would be in the same place at the same time with everyone at once. Everyone I knew and loved was there, including my dad, who had flown in from Florida to see me graduate. It was my opportunity to show him how I had papered every single wall of my bedroom with letters from colleges interested in me. Sure, I was going to USC, but they weren't the only ones interested in me.

I wanted Dad to see that I mattered. I wanted him to see how many people and schools had been interested in recruiting me.

All my coaches were there, drinking iced tea and eating cake. I'd had some good conversations with those men, sometimes I hated what they had to tell me, but I'd taken their words to heart and incorporated them into my life. As a result, I was well on my way to becoming a professional athlete.

In the midst of the barbecue of my graduation party, Dad came up to me and said, "OK, T. I gotta go."

"Sure, Dad." Walking him to his car came naturally to me. I'd said goodbye so many times in the past never knowing when I'd see him again. This time I had a couple reasons. One, I'd learned good manners. Two, I knew presents often came to graduates and I'd be lying if I said I didn't expect something pretty profound from my dad.

We stood by his rental car, a white PT Cruiser, as we said goodbye. Strangers still, I hoped for a life-changing moment between the two of us. Maybe he'd give me keys to a brand new car, or a check to get me started in style at USC. When Dad reached into the car, I could hardly contain my excitement, but that quickly diminished when he handed me a book.

I looked at the title.

Holy Bible.

Maybe he cut out some pages and stashed some money inside. I thumbed through the book and found no empty pages, no money.

"T, my boxing coach gave this to me years ago. I want to give it to you."

Disbelieving, I stared at Dad as if he'd lost his mind, but he continued talking.

"My coach told me there would come a day when I would need this more than any coaching he could offer me and more than any strength I could ever hope to find."

"Sure, Dad." Was he kidding me?

"I don't know when you will need it, but I promise you this is what got me through every difficult situation in my life and I promise you it will get you through yours."

Right.

Just another empty promise.

My relationship with Dad consisted of one year together in second grade, and then some phone calls and intermittent visits over the past eight years.

Sure, I loved him. He was my dad.

But I knew that what we had didn't constitute a relationship.

I tucked the book under my arm, gave him a hug and said, "Love you, Dad." And walked back into the house with a book I knew nothing about in my hands.

Little did I know how profound his words would be when I started my football career at USC.

⚬⚬⚬

Before leaving Vacaville, I returned to Alamo Elementary School. I wanted to see Mr. Truman to tell him that I had graduated and that I was going to college at USC.

Unfortunately, he wasn't at school that day.

I did see the principal, the yard monitor who had collared me so often when I was an out-of-control youth, the PE teacher, and some of the other teachers who had made a lasting impression on me.

I wanted to tell them, "Thank you!"

∽ᗅ᙮ ᕘ᙮∽

Within five days of graduation, I started the process of cutting the umbilical cord. I had only six days from graduation to be at USC in June to prepare for football season with the USC Trojans. I could hardly think as I packed up my room.

I knew I would never again live in that room as a child.

When I returned I would be a man.

As we loaded the car with my two suitcases, all I could focus on was Mom. I wouldn't be the man of the house any more. I wouldn't be able to kiss her goodnight and saying goodnight on the phone was a poor substitute. She wouldn't be lonely because she'd begun dating Bob, a wonderful man who I knew would love and protect her.

But the truth was that I knew this was the moment the dynamics of our relationship would change forever. It was time for me to take everything she taught me and start my own legacy.

Our car trip was very quiet, each of us keeping company with our own thoughts. When we reached the airport I wondered how I was supposed to say goodbye to the woman who had given up so much for me to achieve my dream.

As we pulled my bags from the car, we both began to cry.

They were tears of joy.

Of sadness.

Of pride.

Of loss.

I couldn't see the tears in Mom's eyes through the sunglasses she wore. But I saw the tears as they ran down her cheeks.

Our final hug was brief because I couldn't take it. I turned away from her, picked up my bags and walked away from her as quickly as I could, rolling my suitcases into the Southwest terminal. I looked back to see her holding back her tears.

With my right hand I tapped my chest and said, "I love you, Mom, this is for us." That became my signature move every time Mom was in the stands as I played college football.

As I waited in the B Line before boarding my Southwest flight to USC, I had a moment to think. My dream had become a reality.

I can. I can dream big.

I will. I will do what it takes to achieve them.

I did. I did it. Everything I needed had been inside me all along.

When you dream big enough, work hard enough, and are willing to do everything it takes, that's the moment you step into your greatness.

What are you going to do?

Are you ready to take that leap of faith and bet everything on you? You have permission to dream.

ABOUT THOMAS R. WILLIAMS

As an international public speaker and author, Mr. Williams believes that his ability to empower individuals will contribute to the success of any organization. Throughout his years in the NFL, Thomas R. Williams says that competing on some of the top teams in the league has allowed him to fully comprehend the importance of accountability and the concept of TEAM as a whole. Thomas graduated from the University of Southern California with a degree in Sociology. During his 5 years at USC, Thomas won 2 national championships and 4 Rose Bowls as a linebacker for the Trojans.

There is not a day that goes by where Williams is not preparing for greatness.